This book is called "It All Started with Eve." It was written by Richard Armour who had the temerity to add the following descriptive sub-title:

Being a Brief Account of Certain Famous Women,
Each of them Richly Endowed with Some
Quality that Drives Men Mad, Omitting
No Impertinent and Unbelievable Fact
And Based upon a Stupendous Amount
of Firsthand and Secondhand Research,
Some of It in Books

But you would still be well-advised to read the book.

IT ALL STARTED
WITH EVE

It All Started with EVE

Richard Armour

Suitably Illustrated by Campbell Grant

McGraw-Hill Book Company, Inc.
New York   Toronto   London

Library of Congress Catalog Card Number: 56–10304

Published by the McGraw-Hill Book Company, Inc.

02242

PRINTED IN THE UNITED STATES OF AMERICA

2 3 4 5 6 7 8 9 0 MPC 75 74 73 72 71 70 69 68 67 66

Admiringly dedicated to

ADAM,

whose knowledge of women, if not profound,
was at least unprecedented

PREFACE

THIS BOOK is written from the point of view not of a psychologist, a sociologist, or a gynecologist, but of an innocent bystander. How innocent, the reader can determine for himself. Using all the devices of the biographer, as well as artificial respiration, the author has attempted to make these famous women come alive. If he has succeeded, he may have paid his debt for having murdered Clio, the Muse of History, in two earlier books.

Selection of the women who are the subjects of these thumbnail, or hangnail, biographies was not easy. Long lists were drawn up and about to be carefully scrutinized when lost. One such list was sent to the laundry, and the author was without clean shirts for more than a week. Another was mistakenly submitted as a list of references to a loan company, an incident which caused not a little embarrassment. It is regrettable that the final list of women numbers thirteen. The superstitious reader is advised to omit at least one, and perhaps all.

These are not full-length portraits, the author having omitted descriptions of kneecaps, fibulae, and metatarsals, largely from lack of interest. Moreover, apologies are made for setting each woman in her milieu, from which the reader may have trouble extricating her. Several of the chapters are full of what is called *Zeitgeist,* especially by those who know only a few words of German.

Although an attempt has been made to keep the emphasis on women, it will be observed that men are always creeping in. Sometimes they enter boldly. The reader will understand that it is difficult to describe Cleopatra without mentioning Antony, still more difficult to omit Napoleon from a portrait of Josephine, and downright impossible to keep Peeping Tom away from Lady Godiva.

Great pains have been taken to separate fact from fiction, the reality from the myth. It is unfortunate that, once they were separated, the author forgot which was which. Nevertheless, all of these women, except possibly Helen of Troy, once actually lived. It is perhaps significant that Helen, who was nearest to the ideal woman, probably lived only in Homer's imagination.

Most of these women are what may be considered *femmes fatales,* although it could be said that Queen Victoria slipped in through the back door. In one way or another they exercised a strange power over men. Madame de Pompadour used her beauty; Cleopatra, on her couch, used her position; Queen Elizabeth used the threat of the headsman's axe; Lady Godiva used the threat of exposure. All of them left their names indelibly inscribed on the rolls of history, and the sighs of their victims whisper down through the Corridors of Time.

So immense is the scope of this study, tracing the history of women from Eve to the twentieth century, that there were 7,341 pages in the original text. Responding to the pleas of his lawyer, his publisher, his wife, and his children (both of them slow readers), the author undertook minor revisions which resulted in this somewhat abbreviated version. As the reader will doubtless assume, the best portions of the book have been omitted.

RICHARD ARMOUR

ACKNOWLEDGMENTS

Grateful acknowledgment is made for inspiration given the
author by Jezebel, Salome, Amelia Bloomer, the Merry
Widow, and the Merry Wives of Windsor. These
and many others would have been included
in this book but for lack of space,
threatening letters, and
development of a
nervous
tic.

CONTENTS

NOTE TO THE READER

ANYONE WHO IS TEMPTED TO
READ THINGS INTO THIS BOOK
IS ADVISED NOT TO. THERE
IS ENOUGH IN HERE ALREADY.

CHAPTER I

EVE
AN INQUISITIVE WOMAN

UNTIL EVE ARRIVED, this was a Man's World, and there were no arguments about it. The Sex Question, i.e., which was the Stronger Sex and which was the Weaker Sex, had not yet arisen. As a matter of fact sex was at a low ebb, and it was hard to get up a conversation about it. Almost any story that came to mind was clean enough to tell. No one was ever heard to remark, "There are ladies present."

There were not yet any love nests, shotgun weddings, other women, or small, pearl-handled revolvers that could be carried in handbags. It was, in short, an era of Extreme Simplicity. There were almost no Complications.

It was amazing what a difference it made when just one more sex was added.[1] A French historian, after considerable research, made the following comment in one of the learned journals: *"Vive la différence!"* This is, however, the French view, and has largely been rejected by scholars in England, where it rains all the time. An Eskimo anthropologist, living with a tribe which because of the extreme cold never takes off its furs, put it another way: *"What* difference?" But this also is a minority opinion, with which there is violent disagreement in America, especially in Latin America.

ADAM, THE FIRST AND ONLY MAN

Adam, the first man, had only a first name. It is no wonder he took so little interest in genealogy. He seems to have skipped boyhood, and, never having been an adolescent, avoided the girl-crazy stage. His main characteristic was his

A rather distinguished appearance

relaxed, easy-going manner. He had the self-assurance of a person who had reached the top of his profession, in his case without starting at the bottom.

[1] Never has so little done so much for so many.

2

Considering the fact that he went around with no clothes on, Adam had a rather distinguished appearance. Dressing simply, eating simply, and thinking simply, he merely lived from day to day, not having discovered any other way to do it. Things were going along pretty well, and Adam was not the sort of man to upset the apple cart. He was the First Conservative, possibly even the First Reactionary.[1]

Adam originally had the Garden of Eden to himself. In the summer he slept under the stars; in the winter he slept under a tree. When the tree under which he was living became a bit cluttered with bones, banana peels, and the like, he simply moved to another, where he could make a fresh start.

It is true that Adam had no one to tell his troubles to. But this was no great handicap, since he had no troubles.

Nevertheless Adam craved companionship. He was thoroughly tired of lagging stones at a line and making side bets as to which side they would fall on. He had a fairly well-developed competitive spirit, but the best he could ever get was a tie, because whenever he won he lost. Although a bird watcher,[2] a sunset gazer, a weather predicter (mighty dull, because the weather in Eden was always fair and warmer), and an indefatigable knuckle cracker, he still had time (as well as large knuckles) on his hands.

So Adam built himself a Suggestion Box, nailed it to a tree, and put in a request for a companion. It did not occur to him to stipulate the sex.

THE BIRTH OF EVE

That night Adam slept soundly, untroubled by dreams of women. Little did he know that this was the last time any man would have such complete repose.

When Adam awoke in the morning, he had a strange feeling that something was missing. He checked his most precious possessions: an almost-ripe coconut, a stick shaped like a shepherd's crook, a stone shaped like a stone. Everything was there.

---

[1] He suffered from lack of anything to react against.
[2] They watched him, too.

Then he counted his fingers, his toes, and his teeth, both uppers and lowers. It wasn't until he got to his ribs that he discovered his loss.

"I've been ribbed!" he screamed, clutching his side. His feeling of loss was accompanied by sharp pains. The ether was beginning to wear off.

Eve's birthplace

Then Adam saw Eve. It was a Great Moment in History, the first instance of Boy Meets Girl. Adam was only aware that this pink, soft-looking creature standing by a clump of bushes was a stranger. As far as he could see, there was no connection between this extraordinary piece of protoplasm and his rib, the resemblance being slight.

Adam clutched his side again, hoping for sympathy.

Eve spoke first. "Who are you?"

"Madam, I'm Adam," said Adam, hoping Eve would be impressed by the fact that it could be spelled backward without noticeable change.

"I'm hungry," said Eve, which explains why Adam, who wasn't any too quick, called her Hungry for several weeks.[1]

Eve may have been hungry, but she was full of a thousand

[1] She might have said "I'm thirsty" and changed the course of history.

4

and one questions. Partly she was trying to size up the situation and partly she was trying to keep Adam's mind off his rib. No one had to tell Eve about the birds and the bees. She knew where she came from.

Eve knew all about the birds and bees

While she was interrogating him, Eve was looking Adam up and down, and also from side to side. A number of things looked a little strange to her, and she wanted an explanation.[1] Adam answered her patiently. He had never seen a woman before either, but he decided to find out without asking questions.

By the time Eve had finished questioning Adam, and listening to his answers as if she had never heard anything so interesting, Adam thought she was terrific.

"You're a lot more fun than an echo," he said.

"Thanks," said Eve, smiling. "Now what shall we do?"

Adam smiled back and gave Eve a hand, whereupon they sat down on a couple of flat stones and played the first game of casino. As they played, Adam kept close watch over his remaining ribs. This sort of thing, he thought, can go too far.

[1] There was his mustache, for instance.

5

Right in the center of the Garden of Eden there was an apple tree.[1] It looked like all the others except for one thing. Whereas most trees had signs on them saying Peach Tree, Pear Tree, or genus *Cydonia vulgaris*, this tree was covered with signs saying Keep Off, Do Not Touch, Do Not Pick the Fruit, and THINK.

It became an obsession

Adam had gone by the tree hundreds of times but had never paid much attention to it. He had read the signs and was Law

---

[1] From earliest times, apples have been important to the history of man. Consider the Apple of Discord, a golden apple that made trouble when anyone bit into it; the apple that caused William Tell to risk his son's life; and the apple that fell on Newton's head and led to discontinuance of scientific thinking outdoors.

Abiding. Besides, there were so many apple trees already that he had baked apples for breakfast, apple sauce for lunch, apple dumplings for dinner, and applejack for a nightcap. What did he want with another apple tree?

From the start, however, Eve was interested only in this particular tree. It became an Obsession.

"Why do you suppose we're not allowed to pick those apples?" she asked.

"I dunno," Adam replied.

"What would happen to us if we did?" she asked.

"I dunno," Adam said.

"Will you shake the tree a little and see if any fall off?"

"No," said Adam, shaking his head.

One thing about Adam, he could be mighty adamant.

EVE AND THE SNAKE

Eve became very cool toward Adam. She retired behind her private thorn bush and sulked. Adam attempted to reason with her. He said that if she could sublimate her craving for those apples—get interested in something else (such as him, for instance)—she might get over what was obviously an apple neurosis.[1]

But Eve had nothing on her mind but Forbidden Fruit. All she wanted, she told herself, was just one little bite. Maybe the Owner would think the birds had done it. Although Adam warned her to keep away from the tree, Eve stood under it with her mouth open, hoping an apple would fall in.[2]

One day while she was sitting in the shade of the old apple tree, a snake came up and introduced himself. In those days snakes were called serpents and walked upright and looked people straight in the eye. This snake had a receding forehead and small eyes, but he was slenderer than Adam, especially in the hips. There was a sophisticated, worldly look about him,

---

[1] Adam was a forerunner of Freud, Jung, Adler, and just about everybody else.

[2] None did, but it rained and Eve learned to gargle.

7

A worldly look about him

too. He had obviously been places and seen things. At any rate, thought Eve, he was a change.[1]

The snake bent over and kissed Eve's hand. "You're ravishing," he said.

"Stop kidding," said Eve, but she was pleased and a little embarrassed. A blush started in her cheeks and kept going. In Eve's time you could follow a blush all the way.

"No, I mean it," said the snake.

Eve had never met anyone so suave, so charming. She had sensed for some time that Adam was dull, but it took a little comparison to prove just how dull.

"Do you like apples?" asked Eve. She was sure that she should have started with a more arresting conversational gambit, but this was the first thing that came to mind.

---

[1] The Snake, sometimes referred to as the Serpent, completed History's first Triangle—Adam, Eve, & Snake (Serpent).

"My favorite fruit," said the snake, who, as Eve noticed, had a slight foreign accent. Thereupon he launched into a fascinating discussion of the origin of the word "apple," which he said was cognate with the Old Irish *aball* and came ultimately from the Latin *abella*. Then he made a brilliant comparison of the texture and flavor of such species as the Baldwin, Gravenstein, Northern Spy, and Winesap. Finally he paused. "Am I boring you?" he asked.

"No. Please go on," Eve begged. Her eyes were moist and her mouth was watering.

"But of all the apples in the world," said the snake, "the finest are right here." He looked up admiringly at the apples on The Tree. "You agree with me, *n'est-ce pas*?"

"I've never tasted them," said Eve, hating to make such an admission. What must the snake think of her? She must seem so provincial!

The snake was incredulous. "Surely you are pulling my leg," he said.

For the first time, Eve noticed that the snake had no legs, and no shoulders either. Nevertheless she still thought him attractive, in a Continental way.

"Come, my dear," said the snake. "Delay no longer. These apples are divine, simply divine." [1]

"I might get some terrible disease," Eve protested weakly, "such as appleplexy."

The snake pooh-poohed the idea. (Snakes could pooh-pooh in those days; they didn't hiss until later.) This particular variety of apples, he said, was full of vitamins and riboflavin and would do wonders for Eve's teeth and complexion.

"Do you want to get wrinkled and unattractive and lose Adam?" he asked. "Where can you find another man like him?"

At last, not wanting to overdo it, the snake pleaded another appointment. Bowing from the waist, and giving Eve's hand another caress, he took his leaf. [2]

[1] The snake knew what he was talking about, and it's a pity Eve didn't.
[2] He was a few days ahead of the times when it came to men's wear.

Eve was left with her thoughts, which were mostly about apples.

EVE CAUSES ADAM'S FALL

Why, thought Eve, had she listened to Adam, anyhow? He was a stay-at-home, a local boy with broad shoulders and a narrow outlook. Obviously the snake was far better informed. If he should come back after a few days, and find she still hadn't tasted the Forbidden Fruit, he would think her a fool.

Eve was now standing directly under The Tree. Before she knew it, her incisors were an inch deep in apple. Immediately there was a terrific uproar. Lightning flashed, thunder rolled, sirens wailed, the earth shook. She had apparently triggered some sort of alarm.

Eve was startled by all the hubbub, but even more amazed at what was happening inside her head. She was beginning to know all sorts of things, such as that she had no clothes on. . . .

Adam, meanwhile, was puttering around the workshop, putting the finishing touches on a coffee table. He was the first proponent of do-it-yourself, having no other choice. When he saw Eve running toward him screaming, "Adam! Adam! I did it! I did it!" he knew at once that she had done something.

There was a look on Eve's face that troubled Adam. Something about her knowing smile made him feel ignorant and left out.

"Well, what now?" he asked tenderly.

Then he noticed that Eve had an apple in her hand and that there was one feminine-sized bite up near the stem.

"It's not one of *the* apples, is it?" he asked.

Eve nodded and gave Adam a supercilious look.

Adam was angry and worried. "If you'd just left well enough alone.[1] But no, you have to go poking your big teeth into things. This means hard times, you'll see." [2]

[1] This was not a cliché in Adam's day.

[2] Ever since, apples have been a symbol of hard times. Cf. the apple sellers on street corners in the 1930s.

Adam looked unbelieving

Eve tried to explain. She said she had just blacked out, and when she came to, there was that apple in her hand, with a bite out of it. But Adam looked unbelieving, horrified, and, worst of all, Righteous.

Then Eve broke down and began to sob convulsively, and convincingly. Adam watched her a while, feeling a lump grow in his throat—the original Adam's apple. His tears mingled with hers, and it was also beginning to rain, or maybe it only felt that way.

This soggy scene continued for some time. Finally Eve got one arm loose and, taking careful aim, jammed the apple into Adam's mouth. He tried not to notice it, but it was no use. Breathing was difficult, and he knew he must look ridiculous. "Oh, what the hell," he said, and chomped down.

There was a sudden change. For one thing, Eve stopped crying and begin to snicker. For another, Adam realized *he* had no clothes on. It was a good thing Eve was his wife.

11

ADAM AND EVE LEAVE EDEN

The Garden of Eden, which had been a showplace, suddenly began to look seedy. Thorns and thistles sprang up, and so did Adam when he absent-mindedly sat down. Weeds were everywhere. Worms and aphis began causing trouble. Gardening lost a good deal of its charm, and Adam could raise only blisters.

Adam blamed everything on Eve and her infernal curiosity. Eve blamed the snake. The snake had his own problems, now being forced to slither hither and thither.

Things went from bad to worse. The hardest blow came when the Landlord evicted Adam and Eve. As they left the place, carrying little more than a change of fig leaves, Eve said to Adam, "But, dear, we still have each other."

Adam, thinking about the good old days, said nothing.

☞   MORAL: *Eve was a bad apple, rotten to the core.*

———◆———

CHAPTER II

DELILAH
A DECEITFUL WOMAN

TO UNDERSTAND DELILAH we must first understand the Philistines. Even after we understand the Philistines we may be unable to understand Delilah, but it's worth a try.

The Philistines left Crete several thousand years ago, much to the relief of the inhabitants of that island, and went to Egypt. From Egypt, where they amused themselves by throwing sand into people's eyes and carving their initials on the Sphinx, they went to Palestine to pick on the Israelites. They were a war-loving people, armed to the teeth, and the fact that the Israelites were peace-loving appealed to them tremendously.

There were several irritating things about the Philistines. One was their name, which could be accented on either the first or the second syllable. (The Israelites, playing it safe, referred to the Philistines as "them.") Another annoying characteristic was their closed minds. They were opposed to change, and wore the same clothes year after year.[1] Old ideas, which they had got used to, seemed to them more comfortable than new ones, which had to be broken in. The only thing they preferred not to be old was their women.

Philistine women had one characteristic that wasn't original with them, but they had developed it to a high degree. They were Untrustworthy, especially when dealing with Israelites. When a Philistine girl made love, she kept one hand free so that she could wave to boy friends, take alms, or pick pockets, as the opportunity presented itself.

An Israelite who went around with a Philistine was asking for trouble, and usually got a prompt reply.

SAMSON

Samson was an Israelite. He is known for two qualities: (1) his great physical strength for an Israelite and (2) his great weakness for Philistine women. He also had a phobia about barbers.

Samson's strength was unquestioned. He could lift more than four hundred pounds with one hand. (There are no statistics as to how many he could lift with the other.) He could do push-ups until people got tired of counting. His shoulders were so broad that his robe needed no padding. Year after year he was chosen Mr. Palestine and entered for the Mr. Universe contest.

SAMSON AND PHILISTINE WOMEN

There was something about Philistine women that appealed to Samson, and it couldn't have been their high moral character. They treated him like dirt, first walking all over him and then washing their hands of him. But Samson always came back for

[1] This made it bad for the Israelites, most of whom were in the clothing business.

14

Samson performing in
Mr. Universe contest

more, thinking the next time would be better. He was an Optimist.

At one time Samson was married to a Philistine woman, but while he was away on a business trip, his father-in-law gave her to a friend. This so upset Samson that he tied torches to the tails of foxes, risking persecution by the S.P.C.F., and set the foxes loose in the Philistines' cornfields and vineyards. The foxes blazed a trail and roasted many an ear of corn. The Philistines were plenty annoyed, and the foxes were burnt up. Samson was captured, but he burst his bonds as easily as if they had been ropes. Then he seized the jawbone of an ass, which some careless ass had left lying around, and smote every Philistine in sight, some on the hip and some on the thigh.[1]

Another time Samson visited a Philistine woman who turned out to be a Trap. While they were visiting, the Philistines locked the gate of the city and thought they had Samson this

[1] Many think he should have been penalized for low blows.

time for sure. But Samson tore out the gate and then tore out himself. He left the gate on a hilltop four miles from the city, thus giving ideas to generations of Halloween pranksters.

SAMSON AND DELILAH

But Samson was willing to let bygones be bygones, and was sorry he had let his temper get the better of him. So he went back to standing on the corner and watching the Philistine women go by.

One day Samson saw Delilah. She was walking down the street with a jar on her head, probably doing an exercise to improve her posture. Her dress was long and flowing, the flow being interrupted here and there in an interesting fashion. She looked hot to Samson—and dusty, too. Instinctively Samson followed her down to the well. If nothing else, he could at least get a drink.

Delilah improving her posture

When they got to the well, Delilah took the jar off her head, but Samson couldn't take his eyes off Delilah.

"Ma'am," said Samson, raising his hair from his eyes, "need any help?"

" 'Deed I do, big boy," said Delilah, running her eyes over Samson's deltoids and pectorals. She came from the Deep South part of the Middle East [1] and could turn on the accent when she thought it would help.

"Watch," said Samson. He reached down into the well and pulled up a full bucket with the tip of his little finger.

"O-o-oh," breathed Delilah, "you're the strongest! May I feel your biceps?"

Samson knew he had them, but wasn't quite sure where.[2] So he flexed all over. As Delilah felt his muscles, a tingling sensation ran up and down his arms. Delilah had long nails.

It got so that Samson was walking to the well with Delilah every day. What her family was doing with all that water, he couldn't imagine. He had figured on more play and less work. "I'm just being made a truck of," he muttered to himself.

One day Samson asked Delilah if she would move in with him. It would save a lot of walking, and he couldn't afford to wear out sandals at this rate. Delilah, wasting neither time nor words, said "Yes."

DELILAH IS A FIFTH COLUMNIST

It looked as though Samson at last had a Philistine female who was reliable. What he didn't know was that Delilah was just like the rest of them, only more so. She was unscrupulous, untrustworthy, and underhanded—completely incapable of living up to the Girl Scout Oath.

The truth of the matter was that the Philistines were still hot under the collar at Samson for burning up their cornfields and vineyards. But when they thought of what he could do with the jawbone of an ass, they shuddered. First they decided

[1] The northwest corner.
[2] He wasn't much on nomenclature.

17

to use Guile. When they discovered Guile was busy on another job, they settled for Delilah.

The Philistines told Delilah that if she could find out the secret of Samson's strength, they would give her enough money to go to some place like Sodom or Gomorrah or Las Vegas and have a real fling.

"Are you game?" they asked her.

"You want to know what makes Samson run, eh?" she mused.

Delilah had always wanted the finer things of life—French perfume and a camel of her own. Here was an easy way to make her dreams come true. As for Samson, he had more brawn than brains. His hair was always hanging down over his eyes, and she was tired of playing peek-a-boo. Besides, that time he hugged her and broke three ribs left her uneasy.

The Philistines instructed Delilah. She was to get Samson into a sentimental mood and then worm the secret of his strength out of him, using her most disarming wiles. Once Samson was disarmed and defused, Delilah was to give the high sign and the Philistines, lurking in the vicinity, would rush in and set upon him. Under no circumstances was there to

Delilah had always wanted the finer things of life

18

be a jawbone of an ass lying around the house! Then they found a place where they could lurk and started lurking.

That night Delilah cooked Samson's favorite dish for dinner, a special way she had of lacing wild locusts with honey.[1] After they had eaten, she turned the lights down low, put on a recording of "The Desert Song," and snuggled up. She was wearing the dress Samson always liked, the off-the-shoulders one that was held up by capillary attraction.

Delilah snuggled up

"Samson, honey," she said, "what makes you so strong?"

"Secret," he said.

"Pretty please," she begged.

At first Samson said nothing doing. He trusted her all right, but it was the principle of the thing. This wasn't just another secret, it was Top Secret.

But Delilah kept teasing, and when she wasn't teasing she was snuggling. Finally Samson gave in. A man could take this sort of thing only so long. He told her he would be as weak as a kitten if he were bound with seven green withes.

[1] Locusts were eating up the crops, and it was good to find someone eating up the locusts.

At first Delilah thought he was joking, or lisping. But finally she took him seriously.

"Go on," said Samson, "tie me up and you'll see."

So Delilah went out and got seven green withes, although withes were out of season and it took a deal of running around. Then she tied him up. Samson looked so funny, lying there on the floor wrapped up with withes, that she couldn't help laughing.

Then she went to the door and waved her hand. "Come on in boys," she said, "and pick up your package." Being a shrewd businesswoman, she added, "C.O.D." [1]

The Philistines came dashing in, prepared to take Samson without shedding any blood, at least their own. But Samson had only been kidding about the withes. He flexed casually and the withes went "zing." The Philistines went to the emergency ward and Delilah went home to mother.

But once the Philistines recovered, they were right back at Delilah. She finally agreed to try again. It wasn't the principle of the thing, it was the money.

Samson took Delilah back with open arms, which he closed as soon as she was inside. As for the withe incident, he didn't give it another thought. (Samson didn't have many to spare.) Anyway, he was glad to have her back, withe or witheout.

Time went by. Now and then a Philistine went by, too, jingling a money bag under Delilah's window.

One hot evening, when Samson was reclining after a heavy meal, and Delilah was dutifully fanning him with her eyelashes, she decided to make another try. She didn't want to rush things, but it had been several days.

"Samson, honey," said Delilah, "what's the secret of your strength, really?"

"Promise not to tell?" asked Samson.

"Cross my heart," said Delilah, crossing her fingers.

"All right," said Samson. He would be so weak he couldn't lift a hand, he explained, if she would weave the locks of his

[1] Generally taken to mean Compliments of Delilah.

hair together and fasten them with a hairpin. Delilah, who had been running her hands through Samson's hair, switched to weaving. She had no sooner got Samson's hair braided and held together with a hairpin than he went limp.

"Got you this time, Muscle Boy," Delilah shouted jubilantly, and signaled to her friends. They came in a little more cautiously than before, but Samson looked so enervated that they pounced on him with glee, as well as with staves and spears.

But it was the same old story. Samson had been fooling again and was as strong as ever.

SAMSON GETS CLIPPED

It was only a short time, however, until the Philistines came hobbling back to Delilah with their money bags. De'ilah settled for a sum that ran into six figures, and assured the Philistines that this time they'd have the truth or else, which seemed a reasonable set of alternatives.

So she went back to Samson, asking his forgiveness and bathing his feet in tears. Samson admitted that his feet had been killing him and said this was just what he needed. He gladly took her back when she promised never to be naughty again.

In a few days Delilah was at it once more. She didn't want to wait until she was too old to have any fun with the reward money.

"Samson," she said one night after they had gone to bed.

"Whuzzat?" mumbled Samson, half asleep.

"I don't think you love me," said Delilah.

"Sure I do," said Samson, yawning. "Whatsamatter?"

"Well, if you really loved me, you'd trust me," Delilah said. "And if you trusted me, you'd tell me the secret of your strength.[1] It isn't that I really want to know your little old secret, but if you don't tell me, I'll just have to think you don't

---

[1] Delilah invented Female Logic.

love me." She sounded terribly dejected, and Samson felt a tear splash on his cheek. (It was pitch dark, and Delilah was using a medicine dropper.)

"All right," said Samson, "if you'll promise one thing."

"I promise," said Delilah.

"Lemme go back to sleep."

Delilah promised, and Samson said, "It's in my hair," whereupon he began snoring.

Delilah immediately started rummaging through his hair to see what she could find. She turned up a few things that had been missing around the house—a screwdriver, a thimble, several small coins—but nothing impressive. There was only one way to make sure.

She went out to the Philistines, who were lurking in the hall, and told them to tiptoe in. She said to bring a towel, scissors, and a razor—if they wanted to play it safe, a safety razor. They did as they were told, the last man standing guard outside, disguised as a barber pole. Under Delilah's directions ("A little more off the top . . . clippers on the sides"), they gave Samson a shave and a haircut while he slept.

Next morning, when Samson awoke, he felt lightheaded.[1] He crawled out of bed and began to do his morning calisthenics, but couldn't get up from his first deep-knee bend. When he tottered over to a mirror, he could see that he would have no further use for a comb, brush, or Delilah. While he was going through the medicine chest, trying to find a bottle of hair tonic, the Philistines burst in without knocking. Samson was so ashamed of the way he looked that he gave up without a struggle. His muscles hung down dejectedly.

They dragged him off, and Delilah was too busy counting her money to say good-by.

THE LAST ACT

Samson was now in chains, working as a slave. He didn't mind the chains, but he was beginning to wonder about De-

[1] He had lost about four pounds of hair.

No further use for a comb

lilah. She had two-timed him three times, and this was almost enough to make him lose confidence.

What nobody seemed to keep in mind was that, if you give it time, hair grows out again. The Philistines assigned a guard to Samson, when they should have assigned a barber. Every day Samson's hair was getting longer and Samson was getting stronger.

One day the Philistines hired a hall and put on a show. It was some sort of benefit, probably to raise money for Philistines. One of the acts was to be a few tricks by Samson.

Samson turned out to be trickier than they thought. When his time came, he got between two pillars and pushed and pushed. (One push for each pillar.) His act brought down the house.

Unfortunately for Samson, who had no way of pulling down

23

the roof from the outside, it was his farewell performance. As for the Philistines, those who had come to watch Samson had no further use for their season tickets, and those who heard about the show lost their enthusiasm for vaudeville.

Though history remains mute on the subject, it is to be hoped that Delilah was in the audience.

☞ MORAL: *Once a woman gets into a man's hair, he's helpless.*

CHAPTER III

HELEN OF TROY
A TOO BEAUTIFUL WOMAN

IT IS GENERALLY AGREED that there are fewer women who are too beautiful than women who aren't beautiful enough. This numerical discrepancy has been deplored by men from ancient times to the present. However, when we consider the mess caused by Helen of Troy, we should be a little better satisfied with what we've got.

Helen had the kind of beauty that makes men leave home or, if their wives have it, come home early. It is the kind of beauty that causes disappointed lovers to stab themselves in the fifth act and inspires poems full of purple patches and other discolorations. It is the kind of beauty that brings the blood to a man's cheeks and sets his heart to pounding, often with bad effects on the cardiovascular system.

Unlike most women, Helen looked even better without make-up. At the breakfast table, in an old bathrobe and with her hair done up in curlers, she was a dream instead of a nightmare.[1]

BIRTH OF HELEN

If there is no question about Helen's looks, there is a good deal of question and considerable raising of eyebrows about her birth. Some say she was the daughter of Zeus and Leda. This would be reasonable enough except that Zeus, who often went

Zeus wooing Leda

around incognito, wooed Leda when he was in the shape of a swan. How Leda, who was a normal Spartan girl, could have fallen for a swan is hard to imagine, but this was a long time ago and things were probably different.

[1] Her husband had no need to bury his head in the newspaper.

Others would have us believe that Helen was the daughter of Zeus and Nemesis, both of them at the moment disguised as birds.[1] Nemesis laid an egg, and Leda, who was the domestic type, took care of it. When Helen hatched out, everybody naturally enough thought she was Leda's daughter, since what would Leda be doing with somebody else's egg?

Zeus's wife, Hera, is never suggested as Helen's mother, probably because Zeus rarely stayed home nights.

HELEN'S FIRST ABDUCTION

Everybody said Helen was a beautiful baby. Unlike most people who start out as beautiful babies, Helen kept improving. By the time she was in her teens she was too beautiful for words, and the Greek boys could do nothing but toot their flutes when she passed.

At first Helen thought it was the hot weather that made men stand around with their eyes bulging and their tongues hanging out. But one day in the dead of winter it occurred to her that she, rather than the weather, was the cause of their distress. At the same time that she realized she was attractive to men, she noticed she was losing her popularity with women.

Helen had a classic profile. It looked as if it had been carved out of marble, except that there were no chipped places. Her skin was like alabaster, but warmer. Men were carried away by her beauty, and Helen was often carried away by men. The only Greeks who didn't dream all night of taking Helen off to a romantic island were those with insomnia.

The first time Helen was abducted she was only about ten years old. In view of her age, some have referred to this as an *abductio ad absurdum*. The man who carried her off was Theseus, an Athenian who had grown tired of fighting the Minotaur and the Merrimac, and decided to abduct Helen as a change of pace. Being a Greek, Helen was interested in art, and when Theseus asked her if she would like to see some of his etchings, she went along without a murmur, and also with-

[1] This is according to Bulfinch, a bird who was disguised as a mythologist.

out a chaperone. Actually he took her to a distant isle that was close by.

Helen was eventually rescued by her twin brothers, Castor and Pollux, who overpowered, or at least outnumbered, Theseus. There is no record of Helen's having so much as thanked them. Sisters are funny that way.

MARRIAGE TO MENELAUS

Helen got more and more beautiful. She was terribly in demand, and the supply could never catch up. At one time she was wooed by thirty suitors, including several Greek cloak-and-suitors, none of whom suited. Her family began to worry. Here she was, going on fourteen, and not married yet.

About this time Helen met Menelaus, a muscular warrior who had the additional advantage of being King of Sparta. He was unexciting, but a good provider, always having the royal jewels to fall back on. Besides, he was frequently away on trips to far-off isles, and if not slain on the field of battle might at least drown on the way home.

So Helen married Menelaus. The thirty disappointed suitors each kissed the bride, taking plenty of time about it. By about the fifteenth, Menelaus was getting pretty fidgety. He asked them please to speed it up or he would be late for his honeymoon. When they continued to dawdle, he became enraged, drew his sword, and plunged it into the wedding cake. This started the suitors moving and began a military tradition.

Helen was what is known as a Beautiful Bride, only in her case it was true.

HELEN LEAVES WITH PARIS

Helen's life with Menelaus was uneventful, and that was just the trouble. Menelaus was a Spartan, which meant that he liked to do without. He did without eating, without drinking, and sometimes without underwear in his suit of armor even in winter. He loved the feeling of cold steel.

Everyone thought they were a Happy Couple. No one knew how dull it all seemed to Helen—night after night hammering

A quiet evening at home

the dents out of Menelaus' shield while he stood there taking practice swings with his sword. She tried to encourage him to take his shield to the blacksmith, but he said she was doing all right and just needed to pound a little harder. Even worse was Menelaus' insistence that she sleep on a board, according to the Spartan custom. They tried a double board, and then twin boards, but Helen kept rolling off, and the sound of her falling awakened Menelaus and kept him from getting the sleep he needed to keep fit. Helen was board stiff.

At this point Paris turned up. He was a handsome young Trojan prince, sent by his father, Priam, to visit countries around the Mediterranean on a Good Will Tour. Everywhere he went he improved relations.

Menelaus insisted that Paris come out to the house to stay. "Don't let that art work in the Hotel Acropolis fool you," he explained, "The plumbing is terrible." Besides, the hotel could be cold this time of year, with all those friezes.

Paris was happy to accept the invitation. They would never know, back in the home office, that he wasn't staying at the hotel, and he could pad his expense account. Besides, he liked simple home cooking, having once eaten some tainted boar ribs at a Greek restaurant.

When they got out to the house and Helen met them at the door, wearing a summer-weight robe that let in a certain amount of air and most of the light, Paris knew his decision had been a sagacious one. While Menelaus was putting up the chariot, they had a chance for a little chitchat.

Dinner was superb, and the cushions were pleasant to lie upon, at least until they became covered with crumbs. In the background, musicians twanged lutes, harps, and lyres to drown out the slurping of soup. Wine flowed freely, especially down Helen and Paris. Menelaus, of course, abstained.[1]

When dinner was over, Menelaus stretched and yawned. Not noticing that as Helen and Paris looked at each other the room temperature rose, he asked his guest to make himself at home. As for himself, he had to do some calisthenics and then get to bed early. He expected a hard morrow of slings and arrows on the battlefield.

"Good night all," said Menelaus. Then he marched off, chin in and chest out, breathing deeply.

As time went on, Helen and Paris became quite attached to one another. Even Paris's father, writing angry letters from Troy, couldn't Priam apart. When separated, they would write mushy notes on wax tablets which were melting from being held in their hot hands. But Menelaus was too busy in the gymnasium to pay any heed. Moreover, Paris was his guest and had the run of the house, which included chasing after Helen.

One day Menelaus was called to Crete on business—perhaps to discuss discuses. Packing up his spears, shields, and a change of armor, he took off hurriedly. He would be gone only a few months and hoped Paris could amuse himself in the meantime.

[1] He loved Helen, in his way, and believed that abstinence made the heart grow fonder.

Menelaus leaving Helen in good hands

Paris said he was a man of simple tastes and could probably make out.[1]

No sooner was Menelaus well out to sea, headed for Crete, than Paris began to whisper into Helen's delicate ear about the advantages of life in Troy. He described the topless towers of Ilium,[2] the shops filled with the latest styluses, and of course the theaters. These last were an improvement over Greek theaters, where there was no roof and the spectators got soaked.

It was no surprise to Helen, who wasn't born yesterday, when Paris asked her if she would go to Troy with him. As for marrying him—well, bigamy was nothing to get disturbed about in those days, especially if you belonged to the upper class and could afford it.

So Helen acquiesced, but she suggested that they smash up

[1] He could always study Greek, which he had been working at like a Trojan.

[2] Ilium was a new substance, and they apparently didn't have enough of it to finish the job.

31

the furniture and make it look as if there had been a struggle. Paris entered into the scheme with gusto, always having wished to become an interior desecrator. When they were through, the place was only a pile of rubble, on top of which they placed Menelaus' bar bells, twisted beyond recognition.

Thus it was that Helen went off with Paris and became Helen of Troy instead of Helen of Sparta.

THE TROJAN WAR

Menelaus was disappointed when he got home from Crete and found his guest had taken his leave. When he found he had also taken his wife and gone to Troy, he thought this was going too far. He ordered a thousand ships to be built at once, or, if necessary, one at a time. In order to speed production, he promised each shipbuilder a portrait of Helen. (This clears up the often misunderstood reference to Helen, whose face is said to have launched a thousand ships.)

Despite some confusion, when everyone tried to put in his oar, the fleet set off for Troy.

The war that was fought over Helen (and other undulating terrain) lasted ten years. Day after day the air was so full of spears that it was dangerous to breathe for fear of inhaling one. Shields were so dented that they looked like hammered brass. Meanwhile Helen, who was known in Troy as The Cause of It All, looked down on the battle from a window and wondered whether they had to make so much noise.

After nine years of fighting, the law of averages and a Greek warrior caught up with Paris, by this time slowed down by the weight of his campaign ribbons. To keep things in the family, Helen then married her brother-in-law, Deiphobus, who had worked his way up to the top of the waiting list.

For another year the Trojans managed to keep the enemy outside their walls, on which they had written "Greeks Go Home." But at last Achilles, the greatest of the Greek warriors, rode into Troy on a stuffed horse.[1] Amidst thunder and light-

---

[1] It was stuffed with soldiers, infantrymen temporarily attached to the cavalry.

Helen thought it a noisy war

ning sent down by the gods, the Greeks took the city by storm.

Some of the Trojans fell on their swords; others less clumsy walked right up to the Greeks and surrendered. Deiphobus hid under the bed.[1] Helen, who was only a naturalized Trojan, discovered at the last moment that she still had a certain loyalty to the Greeks. Besides, she had not been married to Deiphobus long enough to think of him as more than a friend. So she told the Greeks where he was.

Thus did Deiphobus learn about women.

BACK TO SPARTA

When Menelaus came upon Helen, he whipped out his sword and said he had a good mind to chop her into a fillet.

"You—, you—, you—," he said, groping around for epithets and wishing he had brought a thesaurus, "hussy!"

"Why, Mennie," said Helen, "aren't you glad to see me?"

[1] It was a double bed, with room for two Trojans to hide under.

33

Menelaus drew the edge of his sword along his thumb to test the sharpness of the blade. When blood gushed out, he was satisfied.

"Faithless wife," he said, glancing over his shoulder at a sun dial, "your hour *est arrivé*." He'd show her that Paris wasn't the only one who got around.

Helen bowed her head and bared her heart, thinking it would be a convenient place for Menelaus to start carving.

This turned out to be a wise move. Menelaus, after staring for a moment, went weak in the knees and dropped his sword. Helen was ten years older but none the worse for wear. And Menelaus could see that, despite all, she had a good heart.

So Menelaus carried Helen back with him to Sparta. It took the reunited pair eight years to get home, but they had a lot to talk about.

Menelaus could see that she had a good heart

Some, who also weren't there, believe Helen was never carried off to Troy at all, and that the whole story was made up by a blind bard named Homer to explain the origin of Helenism.[1] Others don't believe there ever was a Homer. All of this is a good joke on the thousands of Greeks and Trojans killed in the war and the millions of depressed students who have to read the *Iliad* and the *Odyssey*.

Everyone agrees that Helen had what is called "the fatal gift of beauty," and the casualties would seem to bear this out. It is also apparent that Menelaus went to a great deal of trouble to get Helen back. Only he and the Delphic Oracle would know whether it was worth the sacrifice.

[1] The first and most attractive "ism."

 MORAL: *Beauty is only skin deep, and the world is full of thin-skinned people.*

CHAPTER IV

CLEOPATRA
A SEDUCTIVE WOMAN

CLEOPATRA, the famous Queen of Egypt, was actually Cleopatra VII. She thus came from a long line of Cleopatras and
had no need to make a name for herself. Sometimes she was
called Serpent of the Nile, but only by people who knew her
well or were safely out of hearing.

She traced her ancestors back to the river Nile, where she
lost the scent. Her father, grandfather, and great-grandfather
had all been kings of Egypt. You have to go back quite a few
generations to find anyone in her family who did an honest
day's work.

When she was born, it was still B.C., which she thought meant Before Cleopatra. By the time she reached her teens, her father died, and was thus spared seeing her through adolescence. Cleopatra then shared the throne with her young brother, Ptolemy, although as they grew up it became rather crowded. Finally her brother, who was no gentleman, took the throne for himself, and Cleopatra had to recline on a pile of tiger skins.

APPEARANCE AND CHARACTER

Although not yet fully developed, Cleopatra even as a teenager had at least the outline she was later to fill in. She was a striking brunette,[1] as anyone discovered who angered her. It is said that her eyes were large and well placed, one being on either side of her nose. According to Plutarch, her features were strongly moulded. (There may have been a little disintegration in later years, but this was not true in her youth. At any rate no such blemish was detected by either Julius Caesar or Mark Antony, both of whom got a closer look than any of the historians.)

Every inch a queen

Whether or not Cleopatra moulded, we have it on the authority of Shakespeare that she did not wither, which is a more common failing of women over forty. Nor, as Shakespeare says, did she ever get stale. As every man knows who kept her, she kept very well.

Cleopatra was a small woman, but big enough for all intents and purposes. She walked grace-

[1] Most of the women in that desert region had sandy hair.

37

fully, and it was a pleasure to watch her, either coming or going. One historian stated that she was every inch a queen, although he was only reporting what he had been told.

She had variable emotions. You could never tell. She might condemn a captive to death by hanging and then change her mind, relent, and have his head cut off.[1] But generally her demeanor was womanly, and occasionally even ladylike. She could be haughty and proud, and at times was overbearing, especially after having had four children. Her children, it should be noted, considered her a well-preserved mummy.

CAESAR SEES HER

Although Cleopatra wanted the throne back from her brother, she enjoyed lolling around on the tiger skins. She realized she was more attractive reclining than sitting up, and there was something about the skin of a tiger that made hers look better. She told her brother he could have the scepter; she was getting along all right holding a long-handled mirror. Cleopatra wasn't a deep thinker, but she did like to reflect.

About this time Julius Caesar, who had run out of places to conquer in Central Europe, came down to look over Egypt. He may also have been trying to put some territory between himself and his wife, Calpurnia, who was beginning to show the ravages of time. (So was Caesar, but the loose folds of his toga hid the loose folds of his waistline.)

Naturally enough, Caesar dropped in on the royal household at Alexandria. He wanted to pay his respects and to pick up a few mementos such as rubies as big as your fist, pearls of great price, and silken pillows embroidered "Souvenir of Alexandria-by-the-Sea." His palace back in Rome was full of knickknacks which reminded him of the many places he had been. These were the days before picture postcards.

When he got a look at Cleopatra, lying there on the tiger skins, he knew at once that he would have to find room for her in his palace too, even if it meant carting out a few dozen busts of himself and moving Calpurnia to the attic. Caesar was sev-

[1] She had plenty of slaves to carry out orders, bodies, and what not.

eral years past the Dangerous Forties, but he still loved danger. He also loved women about thirty-five years his junior, and Cleopatra qualified splendidly.

Caesar was a man of affairs. After he had finished affairs of state with Ptolemy, he turned to Cleopatra.

"Weeny, weedy, weeky," he said, playfully chucking her under the chin.

"Weeny, weedy, weeky"

"E pluribus unum," Cleopatra retorted. At the same time she let her robe slip a little, displaying as well-rounded a shoulder as Caesar had ever seen, not as yet having seen the other one.

Cleopatra sized up her man. He was old enough to be her father, or even, down in Egypt where they matured early, her grandfather. He had a Roman nose, but what did she expect? There were crows' feet and other bird tracks around his eyes, and he gave the general impression of a man who had been living it up—a Roman candle that had been burning at both ends.

And yet Caesar appealed to Cleopatra. His toga was tailor-made, with a natural drape and a belt in the back. He was clean and neat, for a Roman, and it was hard to believe that during long campaigns he sometimes slept in his litter. What Cleopatra liked most about Caesar was the Roman Empire—an attractive hunk of real estate. If she and Caesar teamed up, they could take over the Known World. She would have preferred something a little younger, but most men her age couldn't even make the down payment on a pyramid. She decided Caesar was for her, and let her robe slip off the other shoulder.

CAESAR SEIZES EGYPT, CLEOPATRA SEIZES CAESAR

While Cleopatra was dreaming of joining Egypt and the Roman Empire, Caesar was dreaming of joining the Roman Empire and Egypt. (It was quite a coincidence.) Caesar was not one to let grass grow under his sandals, which was unlikely anyhow in the parched lands of Egypt. Not wanting her beauty to be marred by a stray spear, he told Cleopatra to lie low, if necessary flat on the floor, while he made war on Ptolemy. Cleo's little brother was a push-over, and in no time at all the Roman legions took Alexandria. Caesar then gave the throne to Cleopatra, and told Ptolemy, who was only ten, to get along to school before he called the truant officer.

Once Cleopatra had her throne again, the first thing she did was to replace it with a couch. Though some accused her of lying down on the job, it was there that she performed her court duties, occasionally taking a beauty nap while watched over, rather wistfully, by a retinue of eunuchs. Nubian slaves, glistening with sweat (they got none of the breeze), fanned her with ostrich plumes. Now and then she went to the Temple of Ra to lead a few cheers. She told Caesar to come up to the throne room any of these hot days and let himself be fanned.

But Caesar never came around, even on days when it must have been mighty warm in his tent.[1] Apparently he was waiting for Cleopatra to make the first move, and he was willing to sweat it out. Meanwhile Cleopatra was thinking of a way to get to Caesar without being conspicuous. She finally had herself

[1] His officers who were in the doghouse sweltered in pup tents.

Surprise!

rolled up in a carpet and carried in after dark. Caesar was surprised as anything when the carpet was unrolled and there was
the Queen of Egypt, reclining as usual.[1] Suspicious of women,
he still expected to have the rug pulled out from under him.

"Cleo!" he exclaimed.

"Julie!" she sighed.

A reputable historian says of the night in question that "they
were closeted together, making plans for their empire until
dawn." Closets were probably larger and better ventilated in
those days.

LIFE WITH CAESAR

From this time on, Caesar was completely under Cleopatra's
spell. She found she could wrap him around her little finger,
provided he took his armor off.

Caesar spent less and less time with his troops, having become interested in other tactics. He got so he would simply

[1] During her long reign, Cleopatra was known as the recumbent.

41

mail orders to his leaders, telling them whom to conquer next. (This was the beginning of the mail-order business.) As for his wife, Calpurnia, he seems to have forgotten her altogether, except occasionally when he had indigestion.

Now and then Caesar listened to the still, small voice of his conscience. It seemed to be telling him to get out and do some campaigning, it being almost election time. But the voice was a little too still and small. The only time he emerged for fresh air was when he and Cleopatra went barging up the Nile in the moonlight. It was a tender scene, Cleopatra caressing Caesar's lofty brow [1] with her soft hand, and crooning such old Egyptian favorites as "Sand Gets in Your Eyes" and "Alexandria's Ragtime Band."

Finally, however, Caesar thought he should return to Rome and pose for "heads" on a new batch of coins. He asked Cleopatra to come along with him, promising her a chariot ride along the Appian Way and seats on the fifty-yard-line in the

Caesar posing for "heads"

Colosseum. He assured her that Calpurnia wouldn't suspect anything, because, as they said around Rome, "Caesar's wife must be above suspicion."

So Caesar returned to Rome with Cleopatra, telling every-

[1] It got loftier each year, the Egyptian climate being hard on hair.

body she was his manicurist, which accounted for their holding hands in public. Calpurnia noticed that Cleopatra had a baby whose nose had a Roman arch, but she thought it was only a funny coincidence, though not funny enough to laugh at. Caesar moved Calpurnia to the servants' quarters and gave Cleopatra the guest bedroom. He was a thoughtful host, and Cleopatra was all he could think about.

Little is known of what Cleopatra did during her stay in Rome. Presumably she did as the Romans did, taking a tour of the Forum and the Catacombs and going around at meal-times to watch gladiators being fed to the lions. She must have spent many hours in the baths, making up for those dry Egyptian years.[1] Homesick for a good sandstorm, she spent part of each day writing parchment postcards to her friends back in Alexandria. But mostly she was trying to break in a new Roman couch. She wished she had brought along her old one from Alexandria. It curved in the right places.

CAESAR'S END

As for Caesar, his end was near, particularly when he turned his back. His mind was so full of Cleopatra that his work was falling off in the Senate. His appetite was also falling off, and his toga hung like a sack. People began to whisper about him. They needn't have, because his hearing wasn't any good either.

Caesar was going downhill fast, and in Rome, with its seven hills, it was hard to stop. A group of his friends got together to see what could be done to help him, and decided to stab him in the public square.

Although he was warned by a soothsayer not to fare forth on the Ides of March, forsooth, without wearing a steel-plated toga, Caesar went to work as usual, thinking he could beat off any assailant with a two-hour speech he had rolled up and carried at the ready. But his friends were too sharp for him, and so were their knives. They formed a circle (the original vicious circle) around him and took turns stabbing. By the time

[1] In Rome the baths were a good place to meet people you had been wanting to see more of.

it was Brutus's turn, Caesar, who had already lost a lot of blood, lost heart.

After Caesar's death, Cleopatra was left in a strange city with no protector, and Calpurnia had a wicked gleam in her eye. But Cleopatra was not so friendless as she seemed. Some-

Caesar and the vicious circle

one got her to the docks. Someone had a reservation for her on a ship about to pull out for Alexandria. Someone had a magnum of champagne in her stateroom. The fine Italian hand of Mark Antony could be seen, especially when he took off his gloves.

ANTONY RELIEVES CAESAR

When Cleopatra got to Alexandria, she checked at once to see when the next boat would arrive from across the Mediterranean. She had a feeling that Antony would be aboard. When the boat pulled in, there he was, standing at the rail and waving his sword. Cleopatra wig-wagged "Welcome to Egypt" with her hips. Antony had to be restrained from jumping overboard and swimming to the dock in full armor.[1] It was plain to the bystanders that this was the beginning of a Beautiful Friendship.

In Mark Antony, Cleopatra had her a man. He was several inches taller than Caesar and a couple of decades younger. He had hair, and Cleopatra at last had something to run her hands through. In addition to everything else, Antony was a finished speaker, especially after he had said everything that was on his mind. His funeral oration for Caesar brought genuine tears to the eyes of the paid mourners.

Antony became the right-hand man of Octavian, the Roman Emperor, and was made ruler of the right side (as you face north) of the Roman Empire. It wasn't the whole of the Empire, Cleo realized, but it was something.

ANTONY AND CLEOPATRA HAVE FUN

It was now an Old Roman Custom to have a wife at home while playing around with Cleopatra.[2] Just as Caesar had Calpurnia, so Antony had Fulvia, a stoutish woman who was always eating bread at circuses. Antony tried his best to forget her, and Cleopatra helped him. He would lie on the floor alongside Cleopatra's couch and sleep with his mouth open. She would drop dates and figs in. Now and then one would go down the wrong way and Antony would have a fit. After drinking a few quarts of wine, he would quiet down and sometimes pass out completely.

There was a boyish quality about Antony. Sometimes he was downright childish. According to Plutarch, he and Cleopatra often amused themselves by going around Alexandria knocking on doors and then running away before the householder came to see who was there. But no one interfered, since Antony was the sort of cut-up who carried a sword.

[1] If he had, his elation would have turned into a sinking sensation.
[2] In Roman law this was known as double jeopardy.

45

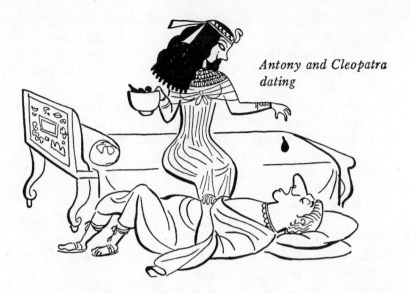

Antony and Cleopatra dating

Often they went sailing in Cleopatra's galley, the one with purple sails and silver oars. Oarsmen kept time to the music of flutes, pipes, and harps, and naturally preferred dirges to polkas. Incense rose from a dozen urns, killing the odor of fish but making it hard for the helmsman to see where he was going. Despite all these refinements, Cleopatra was more effective indoors, when the lights were low and Antony was high.

Eventually Antony said he must go home long enough to retain his citizenship. Cleopatra threw a tantrum, a couple of imported Greek vases, and an ivory replica of the Sphinx. Her intentions were good but her aim was bad. Then she pretended to faint, but Antony, a man of action, had started for Rome before she hit the floor.

Antony was not in Rome long. Fulvia died sooner than he expected and almost as soon as he hoped. He then married Octavian's sister, Octavia, thinking it politically expedient.[1] However he had a faraway look in his eyes, and on his wedding night surprised Octavia by lying down on the floor beside the bed and going to sleep with his mouth open. Octavia, being the

[1] As they said in Rome, "politics makes strange bedfellows."

intuitive type, looked around wildly, but there wasn't a fig or date in the house.

They were plainly incompatible, and the next day Antony took ship for Alexandria. Octavia was terribly upset and poured her heart into her brother's ear. He promised to send the Roman navy after Antony, and to set high tariffs on Egyptian imports if Antony tried to bring Cleopatra back with him.

CURTAINS FOR ANTONY AND CLEOPATRA

So Antony and Cleopatra were together again in Alexandria. Cleopatra wouldn't let Antony out of sight, or even out of doors, and he grew pale and wan. Some of this lack of color was due to the realization that Octavian was on his way with the Roman army, navy, and Octavia.

Every time Antony suggested that he should join his troops in the field, Cleopatra would threaten to kill herself,[1] and Antony, who was rather fastidious, didn't want to have her

Antony squeezing into his old armor

blood on his hands. Besides, he was beginning to lose his military bearing and knew it would be hard to squeeze into his old uniform without moving over the rivets.

[1] She was often at death's door, with her hand on the knob.

Ultimately Antony screwed up his courage, squeezed into his armor, and staggered out to the field, only to find that all was lost. He had lost his army, his reputation, and his way. In the confusion, he reached for his handkerchief, grabbed his sword instead, and mortally wounded himself.[1] In his delirium he said things like "I am dying, Egypt, dying!" not only becoming repetitious but apparently mistaking Cleopatra for a well-rounded sand dune. All the while he looked around desperately for his sword, which was right under his nose the whole time (i.e., sticking through his chest). He became incoherent and hard to follow, but was tracked down by some soldiers who carried him to Cleopatra, thinking she might still have some use for him.

Cleopatra was weekending at the family mausoleum, which turned out to be a handy place. Most historians have painted a tragic picture of Antony, dying in Cleopatra's arms, but few of them will be lucky enough to expire in such a pleasant spot.

For years Cleopatra had been experimenting with poisons, trying them out on her servants to see which would be the quickest and easiest. As time went on, she picked up a good deal of information but aggravated the servant problem. Now, with the victorious Octavian about to arrive any minute, she had no time to order something from the apothecary, even if she could get a prescription. She thought of awaiting the arrival of Octavian and exercising her charms on him, but decided he wasn't worth her wile.

So it was that Cleopatra called for a basket of figs. Knowing Egyptian merchants, she found, as she expected, that there were nice big figs on top, smaller, overripe figs below, and a lot of well-fed asps in the bottom.

Cleopatra did away with herself by coaxing an asp to bite her in the arm and on the breast. But it wasn't easy. For a while she sat there with these parts bared, but the asps refused to stir. She was thirty-nine, going on forty, and seemed to have

[1] If you are skeptical of this interpretation of history, try blowing your nose on a carving knife.

lost her appeal. Finally, however, one asp, sensing that this was his Rendezvous with History and anyway wanting to get the hell out of there, scurried up, took a couple of nips, and slithered off in embarrassment. That did it.

The whole thing was a little gruesome, but this was in the Old Days, before sleeping pills.

☞ MORAL: *If there are tides in the affairs of men, there are riptides in their affairs with women.*

CHAPTER V

LADY GODIVA
AN EXHIBITIONIST

LADY GODIVA lived back in the eleventh century, when almost anything could happen. It was a rough, uncultured period in England, before the development of the bowler, the starched shirt front, and the Oxford Accent. Women were kept in an inferior position, usually on their hands and knees, scrubbing the paving stones.

In those days England was ruled by Edward the Confessor, a kindly old fellow whose only fault was that he couldn't keep anything to himself. Edward was the next-to-last Saxon king, and Lady Godiva was herself a Saxon. It was clear, and will become clearer as Lady Godiva's story is told, that the Saxons were then in the saddle.

Lady Godiva's husband was not, as might be supposed, Lord Godiva. He was Leofric, the lord of Coventry, a town which he owned and rented out to people who were too poor to own a town of their own. When people in Coventry exclaimed "My Lord!" (as they frequently had occasion to) they had Leofric in mind. He was also Earl of Mercia, which was really something. All in all, Leofric was a Big Shotte, and Lady Godiva was lucky to be married to him, as he was fond of saying.

Two serfs and a big shotte

Leofric was all Saxon and a yard wide, with the finest beard in town. Beards were a sign of having reached man's estate, and Leofric had safely arrived. In fact he had been there some time and had settled down, notably around the waist and seat. He thought a woman should be chaste and modest [1] and was opposed to the plunging neckline, except on other men's wives. He kept a sharp eye on his wife, partly for the sheer pleasure of it.

[1] Rather than chased and immodest.

51

Lady Godiva was, by all accounts, a woman to look at twice.[1] She had the blonde, Saxon type of beauty, or, as they said in those days, Sax appeal. She was tall and well knit. (Later she was to drop a stitch or two.) Her hair was her specialty. It was golden-hued and hung to the ground, picking up admiring glances and an occasional burr.

But there were a couple of peculiarities about his wife that rankled Leofric. For one, she insisted on going around the house in nothing but a housecoat of sackcloth from which she had lost the belt. The slightest gust of wind would blow it apart when she opened the door to admit guests, door-to-door salesmen, wandering minstrels, and meandering wastrels. But as long as they made such scratchy woolens in England, Lady Godiva insisted she wasn't going to wear anything tight-fitting.

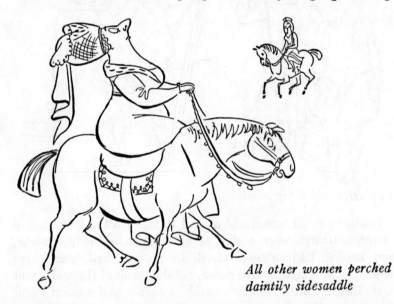

All other women perched daintily sidesaddle

Another thing about Lady Godiva that irked her husband was the way she rode a horse. While all the other Saxon women perched daintily sidesaddle, she persisted in riding a-straddle.

[1] Or even oftener.

Leofric, who had a highly developed sense of propriety, said he just didn't think it was becoming.

"Forsooth," quoth he, "it bodes ill."

"Od's bodikins, sirrah," quoth she, "go to." She did not say where, but Leofric could guess.

LEOFRIC IS A LITTLE PECULIAR TOO

If there was one thing Leofric liked better than his wife, it was money. He spent most of his time in the counting house, and it wasn't because he was a slow counter. He had many pounds of pounds, and the shillings and pence were stacked up in neat piles as high as he could reach. With him, cash was king, and he was only an earl. Sometimes he would flail around with a staff, knocking the coins hither and yon, just so he would have the pleasure of scurrying yon and hither to pick them up again. From upstairs, Lady Godiva could hear the scattering of coins and then the methodical clink of gold on gold, silver on silver, and copper on copper. She knew her husband was having fun.

Fortunately, Leofric had a steady source of income: the people of Coventry. When he felt he needed some more coins to pile up, he simply increased the tax rate. If there were too few taxpayers, he increased the birth rate. He levied every kind of tax: house tax, cattle tax, pole tax, carpet tax. His ability to skin his subjects prompted them to call him, lovingly, "the taxidermist."

If a poor serf had no cash at all, Leofric took one-third of each bushel of grain, one-third of each loaf of bread, one-third of each cow. This was terribly hard on the people of Coventry, and even harder on the cows. But Leofric was unsympathetic. "They are all villeins," he would say when his wife reproached him for his greed. "And besides, what good is money if you haven't enough to stack?"

The people of Coventry didn't know where their next shilling was coming from, although as they looked up at the lord's manor they had a pretty good idea of where it was going to.

They were fed up with feudalism, and would have felt even more discouraged had they realized that it still had three hundred years to go. Their grumbling grew loud, but Leofric couldn't hear it down in his counting house, what with all the clinking and jangling.

Truly he was beginning to tax their patience.

THE PEOPLE APPEAL TO LADY GODIVA

Meanwhile Lady Godiva was slopping around in less and less. It was all right around the house, Leofric said, but he hated to have her gawked at by the common people, and threatened to slice up any oaf who stared too hard. "Half an oaf," he muttered, "is better than one."

Once Lady Godiva said something about going bareback riding. Leofric misunderstood her and was so enraged that he knocked over a pitcher of mead.[1] He finally quieted down, but not before Lady Godiva became strangely thoughtful.

About this time a delegation of impoverished peasants waited upon Lady Godiva. They thought they would find out whether

[1] This minor skirmish became known as the battle of runny mead.

she had a softer heart than her husband. Lady Godiva let them in and then heard them out. Their story brought tears to her eyes, and, clad in a sackcloth housecoat, she was visibly moved. In fact she was almost entirely undone. The peasants leaned on their hoes and lowered their eyes, little by little.

"The earl is a churl," said Lady Godiva. "He is a niggard in the woodpile. He pincheth pennies and biteth shillings. I would fain help you, forsooth, but he is a tough nutte to crack."

Death and taxes, she said regretfully, were in her husband's department, but she promised to put in a good word as soon as she got his ear, which he kept hidden under a shaggy head of hair. They thanked her and took their leave. Also their hoes.

LADY GODIVA HAD AN IDEA

Lady Godiva was touched by the appeal of the villagers. They had a good deal of common sense. And why not? They were common people. Furthermore Leofric had so many coins that he was often forced to count by tens in order to get through in time for dinner.

Besides, she didn't like the way Leofric kept her under wraps. Often she felt the urge to do interpretive dancing on the village green by the light of the moon, and let anyone who happened by do the interpreting. She longed to scamper barefoot, faun-like, over the lawn in the early morning, feeling between her toes the dew.

"Don't," snarled Leofric.

"Dew," murmured Godiva.

It occurred to her that there might be a way to help the good people of Coventry and have a bit of a fling at the same time. So, ere long, Lady Godiva told her husband that if he didn't take off some of the taxes, she would take off all her clothes and ride stark naked through the streets of Coventry at high noon, during the lunch hour. In fact she might do it anyhow, because it was becoming an Uncontrollable Impulse.

"Gadzooks, you'll be tried and found wanton!" Leofric exploded. Then, to her surprise, after a moment of thought, he told her to go ride ahead. He was a shrewd fellow, and he figured that his permission would take all the fun out of it. Also he had an ace up his sleeve in case his wife persisted in this Exhibitionist Folly.

"By my beard!" said Leofric to himself, "I'll show the wench a thing or two." He did not mean it the way Lady Godiva would have meant it.

LADY GODIVA'S RIDE

Lady Godiva went ahead with her plans, picking out an experienced old mare [1] that wouldn't be embarrassed by a nude woman on her back, and getting herself into the pink of condition. After experimenting with braids, she decided on a simpler hairdo, letting her hair fall naturally. She tried several times before getting the hang of it.

Meanwhile Leofric made a few plans himself. When he saw she was determined to pull it off, he put out a proclamation, unbeknownst to her, ordering the citizens of Coventry to stay indoors, pull down all the shades, climb under their beds, and shut their eyes. This way, he figured, the most his wife would get out of it would be a sunburn.

One bright, clear day, chosen for maximum visibility, Lady Godiva headed for the stable, her skin covered with nothing but goose-pimples. The grooms were not around, having been given the day off by Leofric, but Lady Godiva looked her best and needed no grooming. Picking her way through the stable, she began to see the advantage of shoes. At last she mounted her steed and was off. However she quickly got on again and galloped forth in fine fettle.

As she cantered into the main street, she noticed an odd thing: no people. Not a creature was stirring, not even a louse. Shutters were drawn, blinds were drawn. " 'Sblood," she wondered, "could this be Sunday?" She guided the mare into a side

[1] History is mute on the name of Lady Godiva's horse. It was *not* the Old Gray Mare.

street where lusty drinkers usually gathered at Ye Boar's Head Tavern to wash down a boar's head or two with a flagon of mead. Still not a soul in sight.

Lady Godiva rode through every street, byway, lane, and alley in town, with gathering impatience. Not wanting to make a spectacle of herself, she "you-hooed" in a ladylike way and then tried the calls of the fishmonger, the fruiterer, and the chimney sweep. She wished she had brought some bells or a gong. Where were the so-called men of Coventry? What had

She was getting a sore throat

happened to the old Saxon spirit of conquest, rape, and fair play? By midafternoon the horse was tiring and she was getting a sore throat.

At dusk, sunburned and irritated, especially where she had rubbed against horsehair for several hours, she was to the manor borne. She felt she had been given the bird, but it wasn't the gay lark she had expected. She had at least hoped to get her picture in the *Anglo-Saxon Chronicle*.

Thus it was that Lady Godiva came to think she had lost

whatever it was that once had made her attractive. The people of Coventry had appealed to her, but she seemed not to appeal to them. From this day on she buttoned her dress up to her throat and saw to it that all of her hide was hid. Leofric was so pleased that he voluntarily lowered taxes. To make up for the loss in revenue, however, he stepped up theft and confiscation.

Lady Godiva might have felt a little better if she had known about Peeping Tom. He was a tailor who had worked up quite a nice trade in partnership with Jack the Ripper. Being an expert at threading a needle, he could peer through the tiniest crack in the blinds. During Lady Godiva's ride, he kept his eye glued on the street for six hours. As a result of eyestrain and high blood pressure, he became as blind as a bat. All the rest of his life he went around with a white cane and a smile on his face.

The Hero

PEEPING
TOM

COVENTRY'S
FIRST
CITIZEN

Lady Godiva and her husband lived happily ever after. One change was noticeable: fewer door-to-door salesmen and wandering minstrels came to the manor than in the old days. In her later years Lady Godiva reverted to rather careless dress, and it was sometimes said that a few of her buttons were missing.

☞   MORAL: *Ladies who take their clothes off in public may be stripped of admirers.*

———◆———

CHAPTER VI

LUCREZIA BORGIA
A WOMAN WITH UNPLEASANT RELATIVES

IN ITALY during the Renaissance everything was run by a few
great families. The Medici spoke only to the Borgias and the
Borgias spoke only to the Pope. The rest of the people spoke
only when spoken to. They listened intently, however, because
there were scandalous goings-on, and there was always a chance
of hearing something pretty juicy.

Since it was the Renaissance, everyone was freshly reborn,
had a broad horizon, and was wide awake, except after a heavy
dinner. People were ambitious and wanted to get ahead. Young
men, hoping to carve out a career for themselves, carried
swords. Some, with an ugly gleam in their eye, carried rapiers.
All of them were loyal to their families, and blood was thicker

than water and running just about as freely. The only stumbling block was an occasional corpse that hadn't yet been removed from the sidewalk.

It was an exciting time in which to live. Hopes were high, blood pressures even higher.[1] Everyone lusted for power or wealth or merely for lust's sake.

LUCREZIA'S FIRST MARRIAGE

Lucrezia Borgia was a natural daughter of one of the top Borgias, a nature lover. She was born in 1480, and thus was a contemporary of Christopher Columbus, though they went around in different circles.

It will surprise some to learn that Lucrezia was not a brunette. Her hair was the color of gold, and she had a dowry to match.[2] Her figure was better than her face, and yet most portraits show her only above the shoulders. The main trouble with Lucrezia's face was that she had a receding jaw. Even in good times, she found it hard to keep her chin up.

Girls in Italy in those days matured early, and their families began to worry earlier. Here she was thirteen, and not even going steady. It was a lucky thing that Giovanni Sforza, whose family owed some sort of debt to the Borgias, was available. Money was exchanged, a mortgage burnt, and a hasty wedding planned. It was a marriage of convenience, in that the Borgias avoided the disgrace of having a spinster in the family. Nobody asked the opinion of either Lucrezia or Giovanni, but since they didn't know each other, they couldn't have contributed much anyhow.

Giovanni was a little fellow with a large inferiority complex. He was impressed by the Borgias and just plain scared of Cesare, Lucrezia's big brother. Well-meaning but quick-tempered, Cesare was usually to be found stabbing, choking, or poisoning people. When he wasn't in too much of a hurry, he gave them their choice. All Giovanni wanted was to take his

---

[1] Pulses quickened, too.

[2] The illustrator of this book, a gentleman who prefers brunettes, could not be convinced.

bride some place away from Rome, where he could spend her dowry in peace without having Cesare and the other Borgia boys breathing down his neck. (They all ate garlic.)

The Borgias were a close-knit family that kept each other in stitches. They were great jokers, all but Lucrezia, and they wanted her close by to laugh at their silly sallies. So they insisted that the young couple stay in Rome, and that Giovanni come around in person on the first of each month to collect the dowry in installments.[1] Lucrezia begged Giovanni to accede to this harmless request. She was sure he would come to love her brothers when he knew them better. Should they ever be in a bad mood, he could hide in a closet.[2]

Lucrezia tried to make Giovanni a good wife. She would give him the high sign when one of her brothers finished a joke and it was time to laugh. She would hold smelling salts under

Cesare's hobby was tying nooses at night

his nose when he fainted from finding a body in the living room the morning after a particularly rough party. But try as he might, he never could get used to pools of blood on the floor. Lucrezia rarely lost patience with Giovanni, although she

---

[1] Nothing down and nothing a month, as it turned out.
[2] Along with the family skeletons.

thought him unduly squeamish. Bear in mind, this was a lusty age.

When Cesare moved into the bedroom with them, Giovanni got up the courage to complain. What chiefly bothered him was that every time he awakened at night Cesare was sitting up in bed, sharpening his sword or tying a length of rope into a noose. Giovanni began to get purple circles under his eyes and to develop a nervous twitch. His tongue hung out and his hands shook. It was this latter that probably saved his life.

One night at dinner Lucrezia filled Giovanni's glass with wine, and Cesare proposed a toast.

"*Andante!*" he said, lifting his glass. He was a great Dante enthusiast, particularly liking the gruesome parts about Hell.

Giovanni lifted his glass, but his hand shook so that he spilled the wine all over his doublet. He excused himself and went into the bedroom to tidy up. When he found that the wine had made holes instead of spots, he changed his mind instead of his clothes. By the time his wife and brother-in-law came to see what had happened to him, he was several miles south of Rome, just getting his second wind. Cesare and Lucrezia shrugged their shoulders and poured themselves a drink out of another wine pitcher.

Giovanni was last seen off the coast south of Sicily, dog paddling for Africa.

Giovanni sees through it

LUCREZIA'S SECOND MARRIAGE

So Lucrezia divorced Giovanni. She claimed desertion, and was pretty badly broken up. This was because of the beating she took from Cesare for letting her husband get away.

Lucrezia, now eighteen and not yet out of shape from eating

spaghetti and ravioli, passed the time as best she could. It was not a wholly unproductive period, since she had a child by a young Spaniard named Perotto. He was a messenger from the court of Spain, and had to have something to do while waiting to take back an answer. About the same time he became a father he also became a corpse, since, for brother Cesare, familiarity [1] bred contempt. Cesare ran his sword through Perotto, after which he bound him hand and foot, presumably to stop the flow of blood, and threw him into the Tiber. Perotto was left for dead, which turned out to be a shrewd guess.

For some reason, young men in Rome shied away from Lucrezia. But Alfonso of Aragon, a chap who lived in Naples and seldom read the out-of-town newspapers, was willing to have a try. The Borgias encouraged him to come up to Rome and press his suit. Clothes could get mighty wrinkled in Italy in the summer.

Alfonso, also known as the Duke of Bisceglie, was a nice, mild-mannered fellow. When he popped the question, Lucrezia was relieved that it was "Will you marry me?" instead of "What happened to Giovanni and Perotto?" They were married and settled down within a body's throw of the Tiber.

It was not until the next day that Alfonso learned that he had married not only Lucrezia but, apparently, the whole Borgia family. They came to call, full of advice, and left full of Alfonso's best food and drink. Eight people, Alfonso told Lucrezia, simply couldn't live as cheaply as two. Lucrezia replied that she had no head for figures, but the Borgias always entertained graciously and never counted the meat balls.

When some of her family started coming for the weekend and staying all week, Alfonso put his foot down. As luck would have it, Cesare's was underneath. Alfonso begged Cesare's forgiveness and offered to pay for a shoeshine. But there was bad blood between them, most of it dripping from Alfonso.

Precisely what happened in the next few days is not known, but Alfonso got wind of something. It may have been the delicate tang of arsenic in the air. At any rate, one morning he jumped onto a horse and galloped off toward Naples.

[1] Lucrezia's and Perotto's.

But Alfonso was the sort of fellow who couldn't leave well enough alone. A few weeks later, thinking he might have judged the Borgias too hastily and having a tender spot, just above the pocketbook, for Lucrezia, he returned to Rome. Lucrezia was jubilant. This was the first time a runaway husband had come back voluntarily.

For a while all went well, and Alfonso began to think the Borgias were as good in-laws as one could expect. Then, one night as he was walking through the piazza eating a pizza, a band of muffled men leaped out of the shadows and engaged him in swordplay. He played with them for a while, but soon discovered they were in earnest. In fact they were in dead earnest, and soon had punctured his hopes of longevity. He didn't die on the spot, however, but was carried home, where it looked as if he might recover. Alarmed, the Borgias called in their family physician, who in turn summoned his leeches. Alfonso was put through an intensive course of blood-letting and finished off professionally.

So Lucrezia was without a husband again. She just couldn't seem to keep a man. She tried to keep Alfonso, but embalming was in a primitive state and it was hot that summer in Rome. She summoned Cesare, who hurried in from the hall, where he had been stuffing something into the closet. Lucrezia told him that she *must* have another husband, and almost anyone would do. Cesare had to admit it was becoming harder. Word was getting around.

LUCREZIA'S THIRD MARRIAGE

This time the Borgias doubled the size of Lucrezia's dowry. They hung signs in post offices from Naples to Milan, delicately suggesting Lucrezia's availability. There was no rush. In fact, eligible bachelors were seldom seen on the street in daylight. It looked as if Lucrezia might have to go around in her widow's weeds for some time.

In desperation, the Borgias put a large table in the center of the square and piled it high with gold coins. Anybody who would take Lucrezia, they said, could have all that cash, and they would throw in the table.[1]

[1] Otherwise they were ready to throw in the towel.

NOTIZIA

LUCREZIA BORGIA

BELLISSIMA

RICCA

AVAILABILE

Lucrezia was available

Toward evening of the third day they got a customer. It was Alfonso of Este, who is described as being tall, handsome, and broke. What better combination! He had not seen Lucrezia, but he had studied the pile of gold ducats with great care, biting each one just to make sure. (History often refers to him as Alfonso the Skeptic.) By the time he was convinced, his jaws ached and his teeth had picked up some gold fillings.

So Alfonso of Este married Lucrezia and took her to Ferrara instead of Este, thereby throwing the Borgias off their track. They were already, he sensed, off their trolley. Lucrezia's third husband was made of sterner stuff than the others, apparently having a zinc-lined stomach. Besides, he drank no wine until after it had been tasted by a servant, and even then insisted on feeling the fellow's pulse. He slept at night with a sword in his hand. This he explained to his dismayed wife by quoting the old saying, "A sword in the hand is worth two in the back."

By such devices, Alfonso of Este set something of a record: he outlived Lucrezia. One thing that helped was that several of the Borgias got the glasses mixed and drank their own poison. It was also lucky for Alfonso that Cesare was killed on the battlefield, having engaged one of the enemy head-on instead of coming up from behind as he usually did. The Borgias were running low on dowry money anyhow.

LUCREZIA'S LAST STAND

As she became older, Lucrezia went in for platonic love, this being all that was available. She had most of it with a couple of young poets, Pietro Bembo and Ercole Strozzi, who slipped in and read sonnets to her when Alfonso was out of the house. Pietro had a sensitive profile, and would cry out loud if anyone so much as touched it. Unless he was caught off guard, he was never seen full face. As for Ercole, he was lame, and his meter

Lucrezia listened to their
poetry by the hour

limped a bit too. What both of them liked about Lucrezia was the way she would listen to them read their poems by the hour or, if they preferred, by the stanza.[1]

[1] She paid for it by the line.

Eventually Alfonso got wise to all the lyricism that was going on when his back was turned. One day he wheeled around suddenly and surprised Lucrezia in bed with a sonnet. It is not known whether it was by Pietro or Ercole, but it was pretty bad. Alfonso went into a violent rage when after six readings he still didn't understand a word of it.

"Witha ma bare hands," he cried, tearing off his gloves, "I killa dem both!" Alfonso held poets in utter contempt and, whenever possible, by the neck and under water.

Pietro Bembo, who had had some experience with the effect of his poetry on husbands, left hastily for Venice. Ercole Strozzi, mad for one more evening of sonnets, hung around a little too long and was found dead in a dark alley, apparently from natural causes (a severe rash of stab wounds). Some thought Alfonso of Este had a hand in this.[1] But, being sentimental people, they got all choked up and kept their opinions to themselves.

With Pietro and Ercole gone, Lucrezia lived a lonely existence with Alfonso, who had less use for poetry and the finer things of life than ever. As the years went by, Lucrezia got fed up with her husband and wished Cesare were still alive to make other arrangements. She got out the old Borgia family recipe book and whipped up a few corrosive cocktails, but the wily Alfonso suddenly went on the wagon.

At last Lucrezia died, bored to death. She was found surrounded by arsenic and old lace.

[1] They recognized the long, tapering fingers with blood on the tips.

☞ MORAL: *A woman who poisons her husbands slowly may just be killing time.*

———◆———

CHAPTER VII

QUEEN ELIZABETH
A HEADSTRONG WOMAN

BY A HAPPY COINCIDENCE, Queen Elizabeth lived during the Elizabethan Period. This was when Bacon was writing the plays of Shakespeare and Shakespeare was working hard on Bacon's essays. There were so many poets around, all of them reading their lyrics aloud, that England was known as "a nest of singing bards." Anyone who walked under a tree risked having things drop on him, such as inkwells and quarto volumes. Occasionally a poet hung from one of the lower branches.[1]

Elizabeth was the daughter of Henry VIII, a man with bad

[1] All Elizabethans were not poetry lovers.

table manners who threw bones over his shoulder. Almost as great as his appetite for food was his appetite for women. He had six wives, one at a time, but instead of tossing them over his shoulder when he was finished with them, he threw them into the Tower. Sometimes Henry got rid of a wife when she was barely broken in and still had a lot of mileage.

Henry's fondness for beheading friends and relatives was inherited by Elizabeth. A wit of the day called her "a chip off the old chopping block." (He got his.) One of the persons Henry quarreled with was Elizabeth's mother, Anne Boleyn. A fastidious woman, Anne begged for some eau de cologne just before she was to be beheaded, but Henry cut her off without a scent.

Elizabeth was a Tudor, later developing a rumble seat. She took as her model the queen who came just before her, known as Bloody Mary.[1] Elizabeth might well have been called Bloody Bessy, but for the sake of variety the English called her Good Queen Bess. A few referred to her as the Virgin Queen, but without much conviction.

One of the most important persons Elizabeth beheaded was the beautiful Mary, Queen of Scotch, who was actually a Bourbon in disguise. Thrown out of Scotland, Mary threw herself on the mercy of Elizabeth, who threw her into prison. Elizabeth disliked beautiful women, especially nineteen-year-old widows. When Mary began hinting she would like to be Queen of England, Elizabeth had her done away with. Later Elizabeth said it was all a terrible mistake, since she had only wanted Mary moved to a more comfortable room.

"Stupid churls," she admonished her Councilors, "I said I wanted her bed removed."

ELIZABETH IS ALMOST MARRIED

When she was young, Elizabeth was not unattractive. She was a tall woman, proud of her height and fond of looking down her long nose at people. She was flattered when courtiers said that her eyes were like sapphires.[2] What they meant was

[1] The daughter of Typhoid Mary.
[2] Or, when inflamed, like rubies.

that they were small and beady. Everyone spoke of her long, graceful hands, with which she was always clutching the handle of her scepter or the neck of a Councilor who had given her bad advice.

Elizabeth's voice was as deep as a man's. It sometimes startled ladies-in-waiting, especially in the Powder Room. She also swore like a man, spat like a man (i.e., accurately), and laughed uproariously at bawdy jokes, especially those of her own telling. Some think she could have made herself King of England if there had been any advantage in it.

Even when she wasn't beheading someone, Elizabeth dressed fit to kill, spending many a farthing on her farthingales. Around her neck was a ruff, so called because it scraped against her

Elizabeth dressed fit to kill

chin and made her skin even ruffer. Her dresses were of such stiff brocade that she found it impossible to bow. Fortunately, she never had need to.

She didn't go to all this trouble and expense for nothing.

One of those for whom Elizabeth wore her Sunday best every day in the week was Robert Dudley, the Earl of Leicester (pronounced Lester). Elizabeth used to tickle his neck, right in front of everybody, and Leicester (pronounced Lester) in turn tickled her feet, and advanced rapidly. Everyone thought Elizabeth was in love with this gentleman and was going to marry him, but apparently he only tickled her. Failing of marriage to the Queen, he had to be content with odd jobs around the court. Because of his stable personality, he was most effective as Master of the Horse.

Another who found Elizabeth attractive was Philip of Spain. He thought it would be easier to win England by marrying Elizabeth than by conquering it. On closer inspection, however, he chose war. Although his Armada was sunk, he escaped living with Elizabeth and died with his boots on.[1]

For a while it looked as if Elizabeth would marry the Duke of Anjou, the youngest son of Catherine de Medici. She came terribly close, at least close enough to see the young Frenchman's greenish complexion, which was why she affectionately nicknamed him "my Frog Prince." One thing she found pleasing about him was that he was twenty-one years younger. But she couldn't make up her mind. She was still thinking it over eleven years later when Anjou died. Elizabeth never liked to rush into things.

When a Puritan named John Stubbs published a pamphlet about her love life, Elizabeth had his right hand cut off, thinking this would indicate her displeasure and discourage him from further writing.[2] Some believe she intended to have him beheaded but the axe slipped.

ELIZABETH THE RULER

Elizabeth's life was not wholly devoted to leading men on and then fighting them off. England waxed great under her leadership, and became shiny and prosperous-looking. Elizabeth's mark (E.R.) was everywhere, especially on postboxes and government buildings.

Night after night she worked late, keeping herself awake by

[1] And his head on, too.
[2] It would have been a good joke on Elizabeth if he had been left-handed.

drinking tea. Sometimes when she grew weary, she missed her cup and poured over state papers. She was shrewd in governmental affairs and had a political bent, accentuated by long hours of stooping over her desk.

Her greatest helper was William Cecil, the Secretary of State. He was a sober, scholarly fellow who took everything seriously, especially himself. When he laughed at a joke, it was often several days later, in the midst of a Council meeting or a state funeral. But Elizabeth could always count on Cecil to pull her out of trouble. He died in harness.

Lord Cecil usually laughed at a joke several days later

It seemed as if Elizabeth was always having to defend her realm against the intrigues and onslaughts of the Spanish, French, and Irish. England was surrounded by enemies, and it was a good thing it was also surrounded by water. The nearest to an invasion of England was when the Spanish Armada sailed up the Channel and might have overcome the English fleet but for Hawkins, Drake, and A. Gale. Had the Spaniards landed, however, Elizabeth would have been ready for them, armed to the teeth and wearing a metal corset.

ELIZABETH AND RALEIGH

As she grew old, Elizabeth lost whatever looks she had had in her youth. In place of her hair she wore a bright red wig, which helped when she walked in the Royal Forest during hunting season.

Elizabeth liked to be surrounded by young men like Sir Walter Raleigh, her Captain of the Guard. Raleigh was a great swashbuckler, being able to buckle a swash faster than any man around. He became the darling of the court and later of the Dry Cleaners Guild when he set the fashion by dropping his cloak in the mud at the slightest provocation. It was Raleigh who introduced tobacco to England.[1] Previously the English had just gone around inhaling and exhaling English

Sir Walter's contribution

fog, and no one knew what it was to discover a cigarette burn on a priceless mahogany table. Some are convinced that Raleigh taught Elizabeth to smoke, which explains what they were

[1] He learned about it from Virginia.

doing behind the palace. At any rate, Elizabeth was usually puffing when she came in.

Raleigh also introduced the potato to England. He was always wanting everybody to be acquainted.

Several times Raleigh expressed a desire to go off on explorations, especially as Elizabeth grew older and homelier. But the Queen insisted that he stay close to her, and said he could explore at home. It was therefore not Raleigh but Sir Francis Drake who singed the beard of King Philip of Spain. Drake learned to use tobacco from Raleigh, and was teaching Philip to handle the weed when the accident occurred.

Elizabeth eventually lost interest in Raleigh and installed him in a private apartment in the Tower of London, where he enjoyed absolute quiet and wrote his *History of the World*. She may have intended to cut off his head, but never got around to it, leaving the job to King James, her successor. For someone who had fallen out with the Queen, Raleigh lived a long life. Once removed from her sight, he managed to say many flattering things about Elizabeth's beauty.

ELIZABETH AND ESSEX

Just when Elizabeth needed somebody with a fresh supply of adjectives, the Earl of Essex appeared on the scene. Essex was twenty and Elizabeth was fifty-three, or old enough to be his grandmother, as she never ceased to keep from telling him.

Essex was the stepson of the Earl of Leicester (pronounced as usual), Elizabeth's old hanger-on who was beginning to lose his grip. Essex, the Queen's first cousin twice removed,[1] was tall, blond, and handsome. He had auburn hair, as did the Queen, but kept his on all night. He is said to have inherited Leicester's mantle, but would have preferred cash or securities.

Elizabeth took to Essex at once. She liked his looks, and insisted that they always be in her direction. When his eyes wandered toward one of the buxom young women of the court, she flew into a rage, and sometimes into a high dudgeon. Elizabeth could get upset rather easily. People who thought she had an even disposition must have seen her only when she was mad.

[1] Later his head was removed also, but only once.

75

Elizabeth and Essex went for long rides in the Royal Forest around London. Dazzled by the young swain, Elizabeth was unable to see the woods for the trees and often got bushed. As a result of these happy afternoons in the forest she presented Essex with such titles as Master of the Horse, Lord of the Chase, and Clipper of the Hedges. Historians blush to admit that she also gave him the Order of the Garter.

Elizabeth dressed in her finest for Essex. She had large, heavy rings on all her fingers and under her eyes. One of her portraits shows her in a dress with huge leg-of-mutton sleeves, in which she kept handkerchiefs, hand towels, and legs of mutton. In such a costume she would sit on the throne while Essex knelt before her, crying for a boon.

"A boon! A boon!" he would cry.

Now and then the Queen would throw the snivelling fellow a snack, but usually she kept him busy reciting his latest compliments, and this was none too easy with his mouth full. After a day in court, he had bruises on his knees and knots in his vocal cords.

Elizabeth herself was never at a loss for words. She spoke

"A boon! A boon!" Essex would cry

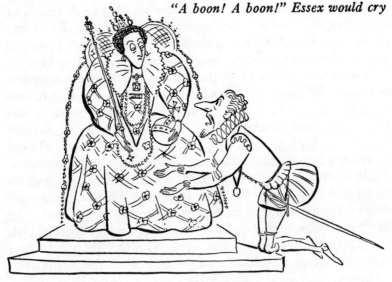

seven languages, and when she wore out one she always had a fresh one handy. All seven got a workout when news reached her that her favorite had married. But the wily Essex spent most of his honeymoon writing a tribute to Elizabeth's beauty. On his return to court he whipped out his manuscript just as her long fingers were closing over his windpipe. After that Essex never knew how he stood, his knees were trembling so. He would start at every little sound, particularly the distant scrape of an ax being sharpened.

Essex tried hard to please the Queen. But one day he saw an announcement in the palace newspaper that read:

WANTED
Willing young man to do odd jobs around court. No training necessary. Personal interview.   *E.R.*

Essex took off for Scotland, hoping to gather up an army of brave laddies who would help him drive the Queen from the throne by blowing bagpipes beneath her window.

What Elizabeth feared most of all was losing her crown. She had already lost her hair, and this was as far as she wanted to go. Thus she turned purple (the favorite color of royalty) and frothed at the mouth when she heard that Essex was revolting. She ordered him to be thrown into the Tower forthwith—without fail and without a toothbrush. This was done at once, or as soon as they could execute somebody and make a room available.[1] Shortly afterward the Queen brought Essex to the Star Chamber, where he held the center of the stage and put on a stellar performance. He broke down, however, when confronted by the Court of Peers, each of whom looked at him with horrid intensity.

Elizabeth might have forgiven Essex and reinstated him as the court favorite, had she not learned that some of his finest speeches about her beauty had been ghostwritten by the Earl of Oxford (William Shakespeare). Essex threw himself at her feet, but got nothing for his pains, which were considerable,

[1] Rooms with a view looked down on a lovely garden, in the center of which was a chopping block.

but a skinned nose. Elizabeth told him that, as a final favor, he could run around the block if he wanted to, but afterward he still had to put his neck on it. Essex lost his head completely.

Elizabeth lived on until she was seventy. This was quite a feat in those days, and was spoken of awesomely as the Age of Elizabeth. To the end, she insisted on being regarded as both the Virgin Queen and the Mother of Her People. With a woman of her determination, anything was possible.

☞ MORAL: *Never be blunt with a woman who has an ax to grind.*

———◆———

CHAPTER VIII

MADAME DE POMPADOUR
AN EXPENSIVE WOMAN

MADAME DE POMPADOUR, born Jeanne-Antoinette Poisson, **early**
in life decided on her career. When she was nine years old, she
told her parents that when she grew up she was going to be
the mistress of Louis XV. (Since Louis became King when he
was only five, Jeanne-Antoinette can hardly be considered pre-
cocious.)

"*Quelle bonne idée!*" exclaimed her mother, who had cher-
ished the same ambition about Louis XIV, but had never quite
made the grade.

"*Bon*," said her father, who minced no words, at least not
the very short ones. He was proud that his daughter was think-

ing of going into a profession instead of a trade. Besides, he was in the wholesale food business, and thought this would be one way to get his foot in the door of the Versailles pantry. The market for pheasants and frogs' legs was poor. Only snails were moving, and they slowly.

So the future Madame de Pompadour put away her dolls and began to collect busts of famous courtesans. She asked her mother how she might best prepare to become mistress of the King. Were there any books she could read? Did anyone give private lessons? Her mother, who had been around but was now staying home, advised her simply to eat plenty of wholesome food, get lots of sleep, and bide her time.[1]

One little matter needed to be taken care of. If she was to become the King's mistress, she would first have to have a husband. To a man like Louis XV, that was half the fun. So, when

Louis liked his mistresses to have husbands

she was twenty, Jeanne-Antoinette was married to a decent enough fellow named Monsieur Le Normant d'Etoiles, who had been taking his meals with the family. "One man's meat," this wit was wont to say, "is another man's Poisson."

[1] In other words, trust in luck and keep her face powder dry.

Jeanne-Antoinette was quite fond of her husband, at least as a stepping stone. *Vraiment*, she walked all over him. Once, in a tender moment, she told him she would leave him only to become the mistress of the King, which he thought a tremendous joke. His sense of humor was vastly superior to his sense of proportions.[1]

SHE MEETS THE KING

When she was twenty-four, Jeanne-Antoinette was about as beautiful as she was ever going to get. She sat before the mirror at night, brushing her hair and practicing her pout, while her husband lay abed, munching *pâté* and reading spicy French novels. They were a happy couple and seldom had words.[2]

It was all this hair combing, and the pompous way she had of piling it high on her head, that caused her to be known as Madame de Pompadour. She was described by a contemporary as being above average in height and, indeed, in everything else. Special reference is made to her round face, a shape that seems to have been preferred to the square or octagonal. She was not only beautiful but talented, being able to turn a mean madrigal, a witty epigram, and a sharp corner. She was, in short, one in a million, or whatever the population of Paris was in the mid-eighteenth century.

As luck would have it, a vacancy developed about this time at Versailles.

The problem was how to get the King's eye, which he kept pretty much to himself. Pompadour, who had been preparing for the job for fifteen years, felt she had all the necessary qualifications; it was just a question of bringing them to the King's attention. Louis had made the rounds of all the employment agencies and interviewed hundreds of candidates, but was unable to make up his mind. Historians describe him as "frozen in a permanent state of indecision," which sounds terribly uncomfortable.

---

[1] Later he was to laugh out of the other side of his face, being ambidextrous.

[2] They communicated with each other in the traditional French manner, with meaningful looks.

Moreover, he arose so late and retired so early that he was out of bed only a few minutes a day. To get him up it was necessary for the First Gentleman of the Bedchamber to use a *lever*, and on cold mornings it was no easy task to pry the King loose. Feeling ill at ease in anything but a nightgown, the King was seldom seen in public.

It was difficult to get Louis out of bed

Pompadour went riding in the Royal Forest, hoping to cross the King's path, preferably when he was on it. She also strolled back and forth past the palace gates, glancing coquettishly in the direction of the King's apartments. She hoped he would pick her up in his carriage or, if he was still upstairs, in his binoculars.

At last, after pressing a few coins into some sweaty palms, Pompadour learned that the King was to be at a certain fancy-dress ball, disguised as an elm tree. She turned up, looking her loveliest as a clinging vine. When the King saw her, *rapport* was immediate. His limbs trembled. He danced with her madly, scattering leaves all over the place.[1]

By the time the party was over, the King had himself a new mistress, and thought he had been monstrously clever to pick her out of all that crowd.

[1] It gave the court rakes something to do the next morning.

Pompadour had now achieved her childhood ambition. She was installed in Versailles, and soon became a permanent fixture. Louis had only one complaint about her as a mistress: she came of the *bourgeoisie*, and occasionally revealed her background by sipping champagne through a straw and munching a *croissant* at the opera. Indeed, when she first came to court, she thought the opposite of *soupe du jour* was *soupe du soir*. But Louis preferred someone who was middle-class to someone who was middle-aged, like his wife. The Queen was seven years older than he, and looked it. Her idea of an exciting evening was to listen to a clavichord solo. (She had to listen to it solo because the King slipped away early.)

Pompadour was a nice change from the Queen. Louis assigned her to a room which was connected to his by a cleverly hidden secret passage. Nobody knew about it but the King, and sometimes he couldn't find it himself. Occasionally he could be heard in the middle of the night, beating on the wall and muttering, "*Mon Dieu!* Where *is* that passage?"

These, then, were Pompadour's days of glory. She had the

Where is *that passage?*

King right where she wanted him.[1] Before long she became the power behind the throne, and anyone who wanted a favor from the King had to get around Pompadour, a difficult feat inasmuch as she wore a ten-foot bustle.

It soon became evident that Pompadour was an expert in jurisprudence, political science, military tactics, art, architecture,[2] and intrigue. All those evenings her parents thought she was out on the town, she must have been going to night school. When people came to her with complaints, she carefully weighed the merits of each case and the heft of each purse. As for the Queen, this poor soul was now living in the wing of the palace farthest from the King's rooms. To get there she had to traipse through the Hall of Mirrors, where she usually lost heart and turned back.[3]

By rubbing shoulders with nobility, the tradesman's daughter quickly removed the rough edges. As far as anyone could see (and she loved *décolletage*) she was now perfectly presentable. It was she, rather than the Queen, who made such important changes in French manners as lifting the little finger instead of the ring finger when drinking tea and the right eyebrow instead of the left when drinking champagne.

Pompadour even tried to introduce soap to the French court, but it never caught on.

A DRAIN ON THE TREASURY

Pompadour was forever ordering a new gown, although she looked good in anything, and a new wig, although her bald spot was barely noticeable. She bought a new hat every day, but wore such a high hairdo that the *chapeau* could be seen only by members of the court who had the foresight to bring stepladders. There was a constant procession of hair stylists and milliners and beauty patchers entering and leaving Versailles, and Pompadour was always telling the King, "Give the man a *louis*, Louis."

Everything was very rocuckoo. But what really unbalanced

[1] At the other end of a secret passage.
[2] She had designs on half a dozen palaces.
[3] She was always discouraged when she stopped to reflect.

the Royal Budget, and the King too, was the cost of architects, bricklayers, and sofa upholsterers. Though the palace of Versailles had about six hundred rooms and three baths, constant alterations had to be made to keep up with the Hapsburgs. There was a steady demand for more trapdoors, sliding panels, and secret passages. The court employed a full-time arras weaver. Pompadour took the lead in a move to build a theater in the palace, and afterward took the lead in all the plays.

Construction was not limited to improvements in the palace. Pompadour was continually talking the King into building a little seventy-five-room chateau or hunting lodge where they could get away from it all. She particularly wanted to get the King away from other women of the court, who thought it was Time for a Change. Their special hideaway was a little farm called the Hermitage, right on the grounds of Versailles, where she could take the King for a weekend of rustic pleasure, such as listening to the moo of cows and sitting in the shade of the old manure pile.

Pompadour also collected art works, especially portraits of herself. This was how she secured a reputation as a painted

Pompadour wanted to get Louis away from it all

woman. Most of the depictions of Louis were busts, but he was a good sport about it. Every time an artist brought him a new picture of Pompadour he would look it over carefully and then make some discerning critical remark, such as *"Magnifique! How much?"*

As she grew older, Pompadour did everything she could to hold the King. She even let him beat her at cards, which he considered the pinochle of success. Although she wasn't much of an outdoor person, she went everywhere with the King, even on stag hunts when she was the only woman. In turn, Louis trusted her more than his Cabinet Ministers, especially his Minister Without Portfolio, who was always forgetting his briefcase. He poured out his heart to her, and his vintage champagnes. He satisfied her every whim, and she was plenty whimsical.

The Treasury went steadily down, the tax rate steadily up. Along with his wild oats, Louis was sowing the seeds of the French Revolution.[1]

Still his mistress after twenty years, Pompadour died of failing health. She had made a place for herself in the history of France, and her death made a place for Madame du Barry. Thomas Carlyle has described her as a "high rouged, unfortunate female of whom it is not proper to speak without necessity." It hardly seems necessary for him to have said this, but he was a Victorian and saying nasty things about people made him feel better.

Madame de Pompadour will not soon be forgotten. Posterity has crowned her achievements by naming a political party in honor of her memorable shape—the Popular Front.

[1] A Generous Monarch, he left the harvesting to Louis XVI.

☞ MORAL: *Pompadour disproves the old saying that the best things in life are free.*

◆

CHAPTER IX

MARIE ANTOINETTE
A FRIVOLOUS WOMAN

MARIE ANTOINETTE spoke German fluently when she was only a little girl. There was nothing unusual about this, however, because it was her native tongue. In fact she started life as an Austrian princess and ended it as Queen of France, thus moving not only onward and upward but westward.

She was one of sixteen children of the Empress Maria Theresa, whose husband is no longer remembered but deserves mention. Maria Theresa was full of homely advice. She told her daughter to eat her sauerkraut without smacking, save the last waltz for her escort, and keep a stiff upper and lower lip. Since she was a Hapsburg, this was no small matter. Marie

Antoinette always listened politely, saying, *"Jawohl, Mutter,"* and *"Natürlich, Mutter,"* and then skipped out to play "Hide the Wiener Schnitzel" with her friends.

She was a gay child who would often lie on the floor and play with her dolls, though she was not prone to study.[1] Her mother would bring books to her from the library, but Marie used them only to press edelweiss and to balance on her head to improve her posture. By the time they got back to the library, unread and full of flower stains, they were always several weeks overdue.[2]

MARIE ANTOINETTE MARRIES THE DAUPHIN

When she was fifteen, Marie Antoinette was considered marriageable, and it was just a matter of finding a suitable suitor. Maria Theresa, who had a taste for French pastry, French alliances, and French louis (the gold kind), sent emissaries to sound out young Louis, the grandson of Louis XV. The emissaries reported back that he sounded all right, but looked ghastly.

This Louis was the Dauphin, and to anyone interested in becoming Queen of France, a good catch. He was next in line for the throne, and in those days the line formed to the right and went halfway around the block. Aside from being timid, sluggish, unimaginative, and stupid, he was likely to become a Great Monarch.[3]

Marie Antoinette had never seen Louis, but she had seen pictures of Versailles, Fontainebleau, and the crown jewels. In order to make it easier, she was to be married by proxy. The wedding would take place in Vienna while Louis stayed in Paris, after which Marie Antoinette would honeymoon alone in Monte Carlo. This would give her time to get used to her

[1] She also liked to loll around in overstuffed chairs, one of her deep-seated habits.

[2] A tendency to carelessness with the property of others remained with her. Years later it was said that she took a leaf out of Madame de Pompadour's book.

[3] Indeed, as a careful reading of history reveals, he had precisely the qualifications.

Young Louis looked ghastly

husband gradually, study French, and bone up on the good wine years.

It all worked like a charm, and the bride and groom got together in France just in time to celebrate their first anniversary.

MARIE ANTOINETTE BECOMES QUEEN

During this period, Louis XV was on the skids and going downhill fast. It was a matter of gravity. For a while the King had lost sleep over the death of Madame de Pompadour; now he was losing sleep over her successor, Madame du Barry. He thought du Barry was a lady, but no one else did.

When Marie Antoinette, young and unsullied, arrived at Versailles, she was shocked at du Barry's vulgar ways, and tried to avoid her. But after all, they lived under the same roof (along with eighteen thousand others) and would sometimes reach for the same *canapé*. Who had precedence, the Favorite of the King or the wife of the Dauphin? Marie Antoinette tried not speaking to du Barry, but the King interceded and told her to say *"Bonjour"* at least. It was only when Louis took to his deathbed,[1] and Madame du Barry saw she might be out of a job, that she started to butter up the Dauphiness. When she left Versailles, she wanted a good character reference.

At last Louis' number (XV) was up, and young Louis ascended the throne. He was XVI. Marie Antoinette was 19.

The first thing Marie Antoinette did after becoming Queen was to throw a ball. (Madame du Barry threw a fit, and was asked to leave.) It was a scene of gay revelry. Champagne flowed freely, and there was dancing throughout the palace. Apparently there was an overflow crowd, because we are told that there was dancing in the streets. Louis had his throne moved into the ballroom so that when he sat out a minuet or a quadrille he could get a good view. An active man, he would have tapped his foot to the music except that he had the gout. Anyway he could transact a little state business, as long as his advisers were handy to tell him where to sign.

Marie Antoinette at this time was in the full bloom of womanhood, but Louis didn't seem to notice.[2] It may have been because she was his wife and not his mistress. She was fond of horses, and contemporary descriptions refer to her fine carriage. The only defect in her appearance seems to have been her skin. She had a fair complexion, but everything else was way above average.

Besides dancing, Marie Antoinette loved horse racing. (She did not compete, but only watched.) At the track she stood up during the races and, being the queen, heard no objections from the spectators behind her. While she was busy placing bets, Louis stayed home and worried about how he was going to cover them if she lost. Horse racing became known as the Sport of Kings in spite of Louis XVI.

---

[1] Where he preferred to be alone.

[2] Possibly he was nearsighted. No one who knows French history would ever accuse him of being farsighted.

Another way Marie Antoinette had of losing money **was** playing faro at Versailles. Mostly the games took place in **her** own apartments, where if there were any marked cards **they** would be hers. Try as she would to win, the persons she had invited always went away with a fistful of I.O.U.s written on royal stationery. Louis stood at the door and handed these **to** the departing guests. Turgot, the Finance Minister, sat at **a** table nearby, subtracting from the national treasury and adding to the general unrest.

COUNT FERSEN

Louis was a timid fellow and always getting cold feet, especially during long winter nights. Some say he was a person **of** great reserve. If so, he seldom dipped into it.

It was a good thing that Marie had Count Fersen to **fall** back on. (She had frequent fainting spells.) Count Axel von Fersen, to give him his full name,[1] was a handsome young Swede from Sweden. He was tall and blond, and the swarthier

[1] Why shouldn't we?

91

French courtiers grumbled about his being the Queen's fair-haired boy. Among his special talents was his ability to massage the Queen's back, which she often twisted when giving someone the cold shoulder. Unlike other members of the court, Masseur Fersen seldom rubbed her the wrong way.

Marie Antoinette was surrounded by dozens of dukes, countless counts, and no telling how many charlatans and mountebanks. But Count Fersen was her special favorite. It was around Axel that her little world revolved. Lords and ladies paused in their own affairs to be scandalized at such conduct. They hastened to tell the King, and he said he couldn't imagine what the Queen saw in the fellow. He never did have much imagination.

Louis did nothing about it except to bite his fingernails. As he grew lazier, he had them bitten for him. Every day he would stand at the window, with a servant gnawing away, and watch his wife and Count Fersen drive through the palace gates toward the Royal Forest for *smörgåsbord* under the trees. It hurt Louis' feelings that he was not invited, for he loved herring.

Smörgåsbord under the trees

92

Marie Antoinette was always seeking pleasure. What with dancing and horse races and gaming and Count Fersen, she had no trouble finding it. As a girl, she had admired Madame de Pompadour's pompadour, and now she went in for even higher headdresses. These ultimately required raising the doorways.

She out-pompadoured Pompadour

and Louis raised the roof. Marie Antoinette was elbow-deep in bracelets, and several accounts refer to her enormous chest of ornaments. Portraits show her with the lid slightly ajar.

These were bad times for France, but Marie Antoinette managed to keep smiling. If she ever cried, she swallowed her tears, using a delicate *vin rosé* as a chaser. She traveled in a fast set, and usually took the corners on two wheels.

Tiring of other pleasures, Marie Antoinette had Louis build her a hideaway like Madame de Pompadour's Hermitage. Hers was the Trianon, where she could try her hand at the simple life. She tried it only once. Dressed in the costume of a milkmaid and wearing only her smaller diamonds, she tried milking a cow into a porcelain pail with a gold rim and the royal coat of arms. She put the pail under the cow and waited. When nothing happened, she became furious and ordered the cow sent to the slaughterhouse. Several of the gentlemen of court wanted to show her what was wrong, but felt they didn't have enough pull.

Word of Marie Antoinette's riotous living came to the ears of the poor, arriving about the same time as the tax collector. They began to call her Madame Deficit, and every time they thought of what she had done to the national budget they saw red. These poor French people, who went around with cheeks pinched with hunger, heard to their amazement that in court circles cheeks were pinched for fun. As they went back to eating straw, a rumbling was heard. Their stomachs couldn't take it.

Some of them had reached the last straw when Marie Antoinette and a band of carefree revelers rode through the streets of Paris in the wee hours of morning (the royal wee), shouting and singing. The people were aroused. When they discovered that it was still two hours until they had to get up, they faced a Grave Decision: whether to go back to bed or to overthrow the monarchy.

The next day a mob of citizens marched on Versailles. They carried scythes, pitchforks, clubs, and spades with which to take care of the Queen's diamonds. They were in an ugly mood, which didn't improve their appearance. As they pressed around the gates of the palace, they raised a terrific clamor. Some also raised signs that read *"A bas, la Reine"* (or "Bah to the Queen") and "Phooey on Louis." [1]

Marie Antoinette was in her boudoir, with three hundred and seventeen Ladies in Waiting,[2] patching herself up with beauty patches. She heard the people crying.

[1] Persons who particularly hated the King were those who had received one of his *lettres de sachet*. They smelled something awful.

[2] She had five hundred in all, but some had the day off. She also had one thousand nine hundred horses and two hundred carriages, having a fear of being caught short.

An ugly mood

"What are the people crying for?" she asked her First Lady of the Bedchamber.

"Probably they are sad," the F. L. of the B. replied with a curtsy.

"*Imbécile!*" roared the Queen. "I mean what do they want?"

"Your Majesty, they want bread."

"Let them eat cake," Marie Antoinette replied, feeling that nothing was too good for the working classes. She sensed that she was making a Famous Remark.

THE QUEEN LOSES HER HEAD

Marie Antoinette's days were numbered, and the number was not a large one. She and the King were forced to leave Versailles and move to the Tuileries, an old palace that lacked those modern conveniences that most hotels in Paris still do not have. They were placed under guard and not allowed to witness the Fall of the Bastille, the passing of the *Ancien Régime*, and other historical sights. The Queen apparently took it all calmly, getting up a faro game with the guards and spending many hours at her needlework, now and then needling the King to *do* something.

They did manage to get out once, hire a coach,[1] and make a dash for freedom. Louis slept most of the way, while Marie Antoinette hummed Viennese waltzes and wondered what ever happened to Count Fersen. She was hoping to reach Brussels early enough to freshen up and get to the theater before curtain time. They reached the border but were held up in customs behind a party of American tourists, friends of Lafayette's. Marie was fit to be tied, and a band of French Republicans obliged. She and the King were dragged back to Paris and thrown into prison. Although she pled for mercy, she was denied even the simple necessities, such as a mirror and a deck of cards.

Meantime the Reign of Terror was in full sway. Revolutionists paraded the streets, singing the *Marseillaise* and frightening everybody with their grimaces when they tried to reach the high notes. Some carried the heads of unfortunate Aristocrats on their pikes, hoping they would keep until Halloween. A guillotine had been set up at the Place de la Discorde, and the people of Paris were enjoying themselves royally. When the knife blade flashed down, Madame Defarge and her ghoul friends dropped their knitting and stood up to see what was coming off.

One day they came for the King. He said good-by to his wife and promised he would be back shortly. Or maybe he said shorter.

Finally they came for the Queen. They were singing lustily, and asked her to accompany them. As she mounted the steps to the guillotine, there was a storm of cutting remarks. But Marie Antoinette held her head high. So, a few minutes later, did the headsman.

[1] It was the Queen's idea to get professional assistance.

☞   MORAL: *If a woman wants the last laugh, she has to keep her head.*

———◆———

CHAPTER X

CATHERINE THE GREAT
A STRENUOUS WOMAN

AS AN INFANT, Catherine the Great of Russia was neither Great nor Russian. She first saw the light of day in the Prussian city of Stettin, and the first sound she heard was someone sneezing, or so she thought. Actually it was her father pronouncing her last name, Anhalt-Zerbst. It might be safer to say that she heard her mother's husband, since some believe her father was a Russian diplomat named Betzkoy and others think he was Frederick the Great.[1] All we know for certain is that Frederick had the rank, Betzkoy had the seniority, and Catherine's mother had the baby.

[1] It had to be one or the other, or someone else.

As a child, Catherine went by the pet name of Figgey, which seemed to fit her better than Peachy. She was a bit of a tomboy, but was encouraged to more feminine ways by a French governess, a worldly woman who had the masters of French literature at her fingertips and brownish flecks of snuff under her nails. This governess tried to eradicate all trace of the Prussian in Catherine, ultimately convincing her that the goose step wasn't ladylike and that she shouldn't wear her spiked helmet in the house.

CATHERINE MARRIES THE GRAND DUKE

When she was fifteen, Catherine was summoned to St. Petersburg by the Empress Elizabeth of Russia. The Empress was looking for a wife for the Grand Duke Peter, the heir apparent, and having trouble finding one. One of the difficulties was that the Grand Duke was a Holstein.

The Empress Elizabeth kept Catherine around the palace in St. Petersburg for about a year, checking her teeth, lungs, and credentials. One tutor taught her Russian and another instructed her in the duties of a Russian housewife, such as the best way to take off her husband's boots and how to turn down a bed of straw. Still another gave her recipes for leftover caviar.

At last, when she was sixteen and the Grand Duke was seventeen, the two were married. Catherine was a beautiful girl with lustrous black hair and what was spoken of as a ripe figure. She was healthy, energetic, and bubbling over with good spirits, preferably vodka.

Her husband, the Grand Duke Peter, was a grandson of Peter the Great, but the strain had obviously petered out. He was small, delicate, and heir not only to the throne but to all manner of diseases. He had had small pox, medium pox, and large pox. An attack of measles had left him with a measly head of hair. Worst of all, he was allergic to *borsch*.

Except for such adult habits as getting drunk, beating his horse, and going to bed with mud on his boots, Peter was utterly childish. Apparently he had had criminal thoughts as a boy, and they had arrested his mental development. Even after he married he continued to cut out paper dolls, and carried a pair of scissors instead of a sword. At least he had no fear of second childhood, because it seemed unlikely he would ever get beyond the first.

The strain had petered out

Catherine went to the royal doctor, Samovar Itch. She thought it might help if Peter had his tonsils and adenoids removed.

"Doctor Sam," she asked piteously, "is it normal for a man to play around with dolls?"

"If you don't keep your eye on him, Your Highness," he replied. The doctor knew what he was talking about. He was a general practitioner.[1]

[1] And not all the women in his little black book were patients.

As soon as Catherine had laid out a supply of paper and crayons and helped her husband deploy his wooden soldiers, she was free for the day. This energetic woman loved all kinds of sports, such as hunting, fishing, riding, and a young guardsman named Serge Soltikoff, with whom she struck up a fast friendship. Soltikoff was stationed at the palace and acted as her equerry. When someone told Catherine to hold her horses, she would turn the job over to Soltikoff. They got along famously, and the young fellow stayed at the palace until Catherine's son Paul was born. Immediately thereafter the Grand Duke gave him a much-deserved promotion and an assignment in Siberia. A notoriously bad correspondent, he was never heard from again.

After Soltikoff came Count Stanislaus Poniatovski, a Polish nobleman. He was a man of the world, a polished gentleman. His buttons gleamed, his eyes sparkled, and there was never any dust on his boots or any grass growing under his feet. Someone showed him how to get to Catherine's rooms by a private staircase, and ere long he was finding the way by himself. Catherine loved to dress up like a man, a disguise that fitted her dominant character if not her figure, and go out riding with Poniatovski in his sledge. Once Peter discovered them riding together, on their way back from Poniatovski's apartment. Peter was enraged to find Catherine wearing his clothes.

"My kolinsky shako you may wear," he said, "but I won't have you stretching my socks out of shape."

Poniatovski suddenly remembered how long it had been since he was last in Poland. As soon as he could hire a fresh team of horses, he set off on a nonstop drive to Warsaw.

Next came Gregory Orloff, the sanest of five slightly eccentric brothers. An Army lieutenant, Orloff is described as having an iron constitution and muscles of steel. What kept him from being dangerously overweight was his feather brain. Catherine loved to stroke his broad epaulets and curl up with his mustache. There seemed to be some sort of understanding between them.

The only trouble with Orloff was that he lacked courtly manners.[1] Under Catherine's tutelage he gained a certain finesse, for instance drinking his tea out of a cup instead of hoisting the samovar. One thing Catherine liked about Orloff was that he was as faithful as a dog, and would come at her beck, call,

Orloff lacked finesse

or whistle. Usually he could be found at her feet, panting hard, just having returned from fetching a stick or bringing in the St. Petersburg Evening Bugle.

But whether a man was dashing like Soltikoff, polished like Poniatovski, or reliable like Orloff, Catherine liked each in turn.[2] "Variety," she used to say, "is the spice of married life." In all, Catherine is reported to have had thirty-six lovers if you count her husband, which would be a mistake.

[1] He was also hard on his clothes, and it was to offset Orloff that Orlon was invented.

[2] Their turn always came to an end sooner than they expected.

Word came that the Empress Elizabeth was dying by inches. This went on for several weeks, since she was a large woman. But one day she finished the job and Catherine's husband ascended the throne as Peter III. As Emperor he was pretty improbable, if not downright impossible. The crown was too large, and slipped down over his ears. The throne was always cluttered with toy soldiers. And while affairs of state were being transacted, he was down on the floor playing with building blocks.

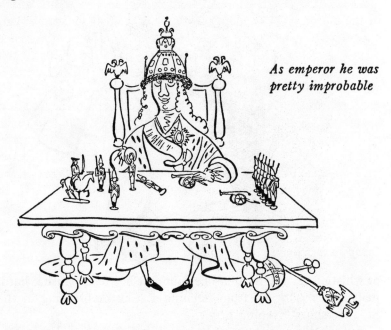

As emperor he was pretty improbable

Catherine decided to depose him. For this purpose she enlisted the help of the Orloff brothers. She had begged them to try persuasion first, but they reported that Peter was deaf to their entreaties, probably because of an accidental blow that caved in one side of his head. There was a playful scuffle, and Peter came out of it in such bad shape that he had to be buried. This, at least, was their story. Some say Peter died of a broken heart after seeing Alexis Orloff, the biggest and meanest of the brothers, step on his favorite toy soldier. The autopsy showed that Peter had a sore throat, with Orloff fingerprints on it.

Once the debris and the playthings were cleared away, Catherine ascended the throne and became Empress of Russia. She was not yet Catherine the Great, but her fondness for rich food would soon take care of that.

CATHERINE'S ACTIVITIES

As Empress, Catherine took complete charge. The first thing in the morning, after five cups of black coffee, she would call a meeting of her Council, and before her advisers had a chance to give her any advice she would tell them what to do. Then she would call a meeting of the Senate, over which she presided with an iron hand.[1] She made, seconded, and discussed all motions, and then, convincing the Senators that they should abstain, cast the deciding vote. (It always came out 1 to 0.)

In the afternoon this Indefatigable Monarch usually made war against the Turks, Austrians, French, or Poles. Part of the time, in the uniform of a general, she led the Army. Part of the time, in the uniform of an admiral, she led the Navy. In spare moments she fretted about the slow development of the Russian Air Force. By the dinner hour she had pushed the frontiers a few miles in all directions, and it is no wonder that several attempts were made on her life by disgruntled mapmakers.

Catherine was her own Secretary of State for Internal Affairs, External Affairs, and Incidental Affairs. She was her own Finance Minister, Minister Without Portfolio, Minister With Portfolio, and Minister Without Congregation. Despite hundreds of servants and bodyguards, she scrubbed her own back.

She was forever inspecting different parts of her far-flung empire, and was likely to turn up in widely separated provinces at the same time, a feat which has not since been duplicated. One minute she would be inspecting a mine in the Urals, the

[1] A great help in rapping for order.

103

next she would be reviewing troops in Omsk, and the next she would be receiving an ambassador in pajamas.

During the evening Catherine would write long letters to Thinkers like Diderot and Voltaire. Wanting them to see that she had a brain, she enclosed X-rays. Once Diderot, the Encyclopedist, came to visit her in St. Petersburg. He gave her an autographed set of his Encyclopedia, and she ran through it in one night, barefoot. Diderot was impressed by Catherine's power. She was the only woman who could lift all the volumes of his Encyclopedia at once. He himself was a puny Frenchman, barely able to lift an eyebrow with both hands.

Catherine was determined to make Russia a great empire. She saw that what was needed was a rapid increase in population.

"We must have more children," she said. "We will inaugurate a Nine-Month Plan."

This, everyone agreed, was an utterance pregnant with meaning.

POTEMKIN AND OTHERS

Despite all her other activities, Catherine still had time for men, about twelve hours a day. When she was in her late forties, she met a young army officer named Gregory Potemkin.[1] She liked his military bearing and showered favors on him. After a visit from her, it always took him a good hour to pick up all the medals and rubles and get his room in order. She put him through various tests and he seemed to have made the grade, at first of colonel and later of general and field marshal. Every morning for several years Catherine gave him a new title and a service stripe. His apartments in the palace were extended to include a Trophy Room.

The Orloff brothers resented the way Potemkin was moving in. Once they set upon him and gouged out an eye. But he looked more distinguished than ever wearing a black patch, and was able to pick up a little extra cash posing for vodka ads. Potemkin did not ascend the throne, but after a while he

---

[1] A brother of Walter B. Potemkin, who wrote *Life Begins at Forty* and *Going Like Sixty at Seventy*.

Potemkin receiving his service stripes

went around the palace in a dressing gown, and everyone knew he had arrived—in fact that he had been there all the time.

Eventually Potemkin began to complain that he hadn't had a vacation in five years.[1] Catherine said she would let him have some time off if he would furnish a satisfactory replacement. Potemkin did a little scouting around St. Petersburg and came up with the following schedule, which Catherine said she guessed would have to do:

Monday:	Zavadovsky
Tuesday:	Zoritch
Wednesday:	Korsakoff
Thursday:	Murphy
Friday:	Yermoloff
Saturday:	Onandoff
Sunday:	Dayoff

Potemkin forgot to leave a day for himself and was permanently relieved.

[1] He wanted to go to a Black Sea resort and paint it red.

In her late sixties Catherine was still in full possession of her faculties, the universities being under state control. She would often invite a professor to dinner and pick his brains while he was picking his teeth. She continued to give many decorations, and her favorite officers were promoted until there were few in the Russian Army under the rank of field marshal. Rowboats in the Russian Navy were being commanded by rear admirals in the stern and front admirals in the bow. This was an era of peace, everyone being too high ranking to fight.

The Russian Navy

As the years went by, Russia kept expanding, partly to make room for Catherine. To the last, her eye was keen and her hand was steady. She could still hold her Council meetings and her vodka equally well. Rarely did she miss an appointment and never did she miss a rendezvous. The spas of Europe were full of her former associates, recuperating.

When Catherine died, she left an eyewitness account of her many activities in her *Memoirs*. What puzzles scholars is how she found time to jot things down.

☞ MORAL: *Women like Catherine the Great are few and far between, which is perhaps just as well.*

CHAPTER XI

JOSEPHINE
AN UNPRODUCTIVE WOMAN

JOSEPHINE WAS the daughter of a Creole planter in Martinique, and as a girl helped her father plant Creoles. Her maiden name was Marie-Joseph-Rose Tascher de la Pagerie, and it is no wonder that as soon as she was old enough she went to Paris to see what could be done about it.

In Paris, she married the Viscount Alexandre de Beauharnais, who was taken by her beauty. When he discovered how he had been taken, he enlisted in the Army and applied for foreign duty. During the French Revolution he was guillotined because he had noble blood, which the common people were now seeing in quantity for the first time. His decapitation left

Josephine with two children, Eugene and Horsense, but without the head of the family.

In appearance Josephine was slender and dark, with straight black hair and a small mouth. She was a sophisticated coquette, thoroughly schooled in the *double-entendre* and the double negative. Despite her coquettishness she was cold and not easily aroused, especially on winter mornings. She had a certain attractiveness withal (withal the rouge she used), and wore a haunting perfume from Martinique that had a tendency to asphyxiate her lovers.

As the widow of the Viscount de Beauharnais, she cut a wide swath in Paris society, using a bolo knife that she had learned to handle in Martinique. Known as a woman of high style, she established the fashion for a flowing gown with the waist just under the armpits. This ultimately lost its vogue for general wear, but is still favored by designers of maternity dresses. At gatherings of the *haut monde*, Josephine was sure to be among the merrymakers, busily making merry.

She was, indeed, an eligible young widow, having a private income and a private phone which was listed in the Directory. It was true that the leaders of France with whom she consorted in the fashionable *salons* were the bloodstained wretches who had executed her husband, but the splotches on their sleeves had faded until they could be seen only through a high-powered lorgnette. What Josephine sought was a husband to look after her two children.[1] Little did she know that her husband would have his hands full tidying up an Empire.

Fate was weaving her web.

ENTER NAPOLEON

Napoleon Bonaparte at this time was a general in the French Army. He had come a long way, having started about six hundred miles to the south, in Corsica.[2]

Already he had proved himself an able strategist, having

[1] Parisian baby sitters were highly unreliable after the Revolution.

[2] Josephine and Napoleon were both born on islands, a fact which is fraught with insignificance.

maneuvered from corporal to general without wasting time as a buck sergeant. He had uncanny powers. He could tell which way the tide of battle was going without getting his feet wet. He knew when his star had risen, even in the daytime. And he could not only read a military map while at a full gallop but fold it up again before the battle was over. The most remarkable thing, as his pictures reveal, was that he performed all these exploits with one hand.

What Napoleon needed was a woman of considerable station. He was obviously a young man who was going far, and he wanted a place to check his bags. When he met Josephine, he thought this comely widow was exactly what he needed. She, for her part, was impressed by the ardor of his suit, which included a swallow-tailed coat and skin-tight pants. Napoleon

Their nuptials were immediate

impetuously insisted that their nuptials be immediate. Once married, he thought of enlisting in the Army, like Beauharnais, and then remembered that he was already in. More than that, he was a general, and he thanked his lucky stars.

109

They had been married only a couple of days when Napoleon said he was sorry, but he had an engagement. He had to lead the Army into Italy.[1] He promised Josephine he would come home as soon as the Italian campaign was over. (This was the first of Napoleon's many campaign promises.) Then he left in such a hurry that he was still buttoning up his vest and pinning on medals as he galloped off. Josephine had crammed his hat onto his head at the last minute, and in her haste had put it on sideways. In loving remembrance of his bride, Napoleon never turned it around the right way. No one dared laugh.

Why Napoleon left so hurriedly is not known. According to one account, he got "a whiff of grapeshot," a smell which, as an artilleryman, he couldn't resist. Others believe that he was in a hurry to wind up the Italian campaign before the rainy season, being fearful lest his epaulets shrink.[2]

Be that as it may, Napoleon was across the border into Italy before Josephine's wedding bouquet had wilted.

THEIR LOVE LETTERS

Josephine was six years older than her husband, but Napoleon was not easily intimidated. She might have seniority, but he outranked her. Also he was taller than she when he sat on a horse, which he did as much as possible, even taking his meals on a tray.

"*Absence*," as the great Roussaire once wrote, "makes *le coeur* grow *fondeur*." When off on a campaign, Napoleon could see Josephine only in his mind's eye, in which he didn't have quite 20/20 vision. She looked good to him from Italy and even better from Egypt. He counted the days until the war would be over and he could rejoin his beloved.

As for Josephine, she had barely gone inside the house after waving good-by when she received her first letter from Napoleon. He had written it while riding off down the street at the head of his troops, and had dropped it into the mailbox at the

[1] Josephine thought there must surely be *someone* else who knew the way.

[2] Still others contend that he went to Italy for fresh laurels, but there is little reliable evidence that he was a flower lover.

corner. It was full of hot-blooded Corsican passion which seeped out of the envelope and gave the paper a slightly charred look. This first letter, which was to be followed within ten minutes by another, read as follows:

Ma chère *Josephine:*

How I miss you! It seems like ages since we were locked in an embrace, unable to find the key. I am already sick of this war and the anticipation of six months of ravioli, but Destiny impels me ever onward. Do you miss me? I hope the enemy artillery does. Write me in care of General Delivery, who can be trusted not to steam open your letters. Herewith a million kisses, more to follow.

Nappy

Every day Napoleon wrote Josephine a letter, and every day he looked for one from her. When the courier arrived, Napoleon desperately pawed through the pile of state papers, peace treaties, and official letters relieving him of his command, looking for a note, a word from Josephine. Day after day, *rien.*

"Chère Josephine"

With shells screaming overhead [1] and generals screaming alongside, Napoleon continued to write his daily letter to his

[1] He rarely had to duck, being so short already. He was born that way; the rumor that he shrank from encounter with the enemy is entirely unfounded.

111

wife. After a year or so of receiving no reply, his epistles began to lack some of their accustomed fervor. The following was written in Venice on July 8, 1796, shortly after Napoleon swam his horse up the Grand Canal while tasting the fruits [1] of victory.

Chère *Josephine:*
> *Having wonderful time. Wish you were her. Why don't you write? Captured fifty thousand Austrians today. Regret enclosing only a thousand kisses, but am suffering from battle fatigue and a bad case of chapped lips.*
>
> *Napoleon*

Still no word from Josephine. Napoleon was beginning to think he had married a Bad Correspondent. A sad letter, revealing his unhappiness and confusion, is the following, written after his horse was shot from under him and he took the bit in his teeth, spurring himself onward into battle:

Josephine:
> *Should appreciate hearing from you. Captured ten thousand kisses today. Enclosed are a thousand Austrians.*
>
> *N.B.*

The reason Josephine didn't write was that she was too busy. While Napoleon was making advances in Italy, a young French hussar [2] by the name of Hippolyte Charles was making advances in Paris. He was a dandy, with well-turned legs which were screwed tightly into his knee sockets. Josephine and Hippolyte were often seen dancing at Parisian hot spots. According to rumor, they once danced in the nude, probably when Josephine said she hadn't a thing to wear and Hippolyte gallantly joined her so that she wouldn't be conspicuous.

At any rate, Josephine found Hippo amusing and also distracting. Many a day she would sit down to write Napoleon a letter. But just as she finished sharpening her quills and

[1] In this case, grapes.
[2] Also described as a *chasseur*, or chaser.

collecting her wits (or vice versa), there would be a knock on the door. Later Hippo came in without knocking, but it interfered with letter writing just as much.

"*Ça ne fait rien,*" said Josephine. "I'll write tomorrow." She had the best intentions, but always believed in doing first things first.

By the time she finally got around to writing, Napoleon had won a dozen battles and slouched back to France, encrusted with medals and heavy with honors. He came unannounced, wanting to surprise Josephine.[1] As he rode up the street and dismounted at the front door, Josephine had just finished writing "*Mon cher* Napoleon—" and Hippolyte had just finished vaulting the back fence. He was last heard of in French Equatorial Africa, trying to sell his memoirs to a Ubangi publisher.

EMPRESS OF FRANCE

What annoyed Napoleon, when he returned to Paris, was that everyone was impressed with his victories but Josephine.

"Just think of it, *chérie,*" he said. "I've captured a hundred and fifty thousand prisoners, two hundred standards, four hundred substandards, and twenty-seven cases of Rhine wine, 1792.[2] I've also captured twenty paintings by Titian, four by Botticelli, and—"

"Must you always talk shop?" Josephine pouted. Then she yawned in his face. She might at least have put her hand over her mouth.

This was too much for the patient Napoleon. So she wasn't even a good listener! And he knew all about her infidelity. The word had been brought to him by an aide-de-camp while he was spending the weekend with the wife of one of his officers. He was shocked. When he told Josephine what he knew, she shrugged her shoulders.

"*C'est la vie,*" she said.

Napoleon was infuriated. If there was anything he hated it was a cliché. He berated her for not writing, and accused her of hoarding postage stamps. Why had she never sent his clean

[1] With Hippolyte.
[2] A good year, very dry.

laundry or his elevator shoes? He had been humiliated, accepting the surrender of the King of Sardinia in a dirty tunic.

It turned out that Josephine had never read any of Napoleon's letters. She had looked all over, she said, but couldn't find a letter opener. The final indignity occurred when Josephine insisted that her wire-haired lap dog, Fortuné, sleep in bed with them. Fortuné and Napoleon never cared for one another.

Nonetheless, when he was crowned Emperor, he crowned Josephine Empress of France, and did it more gently than might have been expected. She might be unfaithful and a poor correspondent, but she had an enormous amount of what he called *je ne sais quoi*.[1]

JOSEPHINE FIZZLES OUT

Josephine gave Napoleon a certain amount of companionship, but her chief function was to produce an heir. The Emperor *had* to have someone to carry on the name, what with that big "N" on all the towels, napkins, and brandy glasses.

So he tried to overlook her shortcomings,[2] and hurled gifts at her feet until she was hardly able to walk. He gave her dresses imported from Paris (living there made it easy), diamonds studded with diamonds, and a charm bracelet. All he wanted from her was a son. "But I've *done* that," was her answer. Josephine had had a son by her marriage with Beauharnais, and didn't see why he wouldn't do. But Napoleon wouldn't settle for anything secondhand. He bore her no ill will, but it didn't seem right that she bore him no son.

Shortly afterwards Josephine began to put on weight, and Napoleon was delighted. It seemed that his fondest dreams were about to be fulfilled. But as the years went by and she simply grew heavier, he grew discouraged.

"My union is without issue,"[3] he was heard to grumble in the classical argot of the day.

[1] "I do not know what," which the French have been good at not knowing ever since.

[2] Which he did by standing on his tiptoes.

[3] Years later, when the son he eventually got refused to marry, the Emperor was heard to grumble, "My issue is without union." He was a *very* hard man to satisfy.

Napoleon began to give up hope. Historians say that a cloud sat upon his brow. The court physician was no help, and neither was a meteorologist. Napoleon begged Josephine to have just one son, a little five- or six-pounder would do. He teased, he cajoled, he threatened. Finally he gave her a deadline: if she didn't have a son by such-and-such a date, he would have to divorce her and find someone who was more co-operative.

The deadline came and went. Napoleon gave her another ten days. Then he gave her an extra twenty-four hours. At last he gave her the gate. Thereupon he married Marie Louise of Austria, a considerate woman who bore him a son the moment he asked. Napoleon triumphantly took the baby around to Malmaison to show Josephine.

"What is it?" she asked.

"A baby," said Napoleon. Then, catching the intent of her question, he added, *"Un garçon."*

"Why, Nappy," she exulted, never one to hold grudges, "another little corporal!"

"Corporal, nonsense," Napoleon snorted. "This is the King of Rome!"

He strutted around the place, looking inches taller than usual, which enabled him to stare Josephine straight in the eye. And he had *both* hands stuck into his vest.

Then, carrying the baby at Right Shoulder Arms, he marched out. Before he left, he gave Josephine a cigar.

☞ MORAL: *A woman who can't give a man anything but the best years of her life should be glad she isn't married to Napoleon.*

———◆———

CHAPTER XII

QUEEN VICTORIA
A PROPER WOMAN

IN 1819, when Victoria was born, George III was mad. We don't know what about. Maybe it was because, although he was the King, England was actually run by the Prince Regent, a gentleman who was fond of the out-of-doors and gave his name to Regent's Park. He also gave his name to Regent Street. This type of generosity [1] was to become a characteristic of the Victorian Era.

Victoria was christened Alexandrina Victoria to please the Emperor Alexander of Russia, who was worth pleasing. She was the daughter of the Duke of Kent and the Princess of

[1] An inexpensive type.

117

Saxe-Coburg. The Duke of Kent was the fourth son of George III,[1] and it hardly seemed worthwhile for him to marry and have children, since his older brothers stood between him and the throne. (They refused to give him even a look.) But he had a strong sense of duty and went ahead and got married, although he was sullen about it.

As a girl, Victoria was taught to be strait-laced, strait-faced, and aware of her position, which was usually on the edge of her chair. There was always a chance she might become the Queen, and she could at least become one hundred per cent British and able to wear tweeds without scratching in public.

Victoria's father died of wet feet, and other members of the royal family fared no better. The crowd around the throne suddenly thinned out. When her uncle, King William IV, died, Victoria found herself next in the line of succession.[2]

She was still in bed, however, when in the early hours of the morning the Archbishop of Canterbury and the Lord Chamber-

"Who, me?"

lain arrived at Kensington with the news. They rang the bell and knocked and huzzaed, but were left cooling their heels. At last they were shown into Victoria's presence. They told her she was the Queen, and she was glad.

[1] Or was it the third son of George IV?

[2] Which led to the famous expression, "If at first you don't succeed, just wait for a few deaths in the family."

118

She was glad, that is, that they kneeled face down, since her hair was in curlers and her feet were in bedroom slippers. She was covered with blushes (and a nightgown) and asked them please to keep their eyes closed when they got up. It was a bad start, especially for the Victorian Era.

As soon as the Archbishop and the Lord Chamberlain departed, Victoria gave her first order as Queen. She had been sleeping with her mother all these years, and now she demanded a bed of her own. Her mother wept and wailed about losing her baby,[1] but consented when she was promised a hot-water bottle.

Victoria was a good little girl. Later she became a good big girl, and finally a good old woman. As Queen, she set the moral tone, and even bad people went around being good. This led to the expression, "too much of a good thing." [2] It also led to a flourishing trade in bootlegged portraits of du Barry and Pompadour, which found their way into the private den of many a bluff and hearty Englishman.

VICTORIA BEGINS HER REIGN

Thus the Good Things of Life came to Victoria when she was still young enough to enjoy them. She ascended the throne with youthful enthusiasm, but wearing a long skirt to make sure her ankles didn't show. Portraits of her at this time reveal that she was short and slender, and she remained short all her life. She had a small mouth, which she could purse at the drop of a "darn" or an "infernal."

Shortly after she became Queen, Victoria moved from Kensington to Buckingham Palace, where she could watch the Changing of the Guard and see that there was no shortchanging. She also had a view of London from her window and could keep track of people going in and out of pubs. She was unhappy about English drinking habits. Although she reigned, she never poured.[3]

[1] Victoria was barely eighteen.

[2] But it was not too good to last, for Victoria ruled almost sixty-four years.

[3] She also disapproved of smoking, thinking it rude of people to smoke in her presence and sneaky of them to smoke in her absence.

In politics, Victoria was a Whig, which means that she was less opposed to change than if she had been a Tory. Reform was in the air, and although the English kept their windows closed, some of it seeped in. As a young Queen, Victoria was fond of her Prime Minister, Lord Melbourne, a Conservative Liberal who was bitterly opposed to the Liberal Conservatives. He was an old dog who, when he was around the Queen, was inclined to be kittenish. Melbourne kept her informed about state business, whispered such court gossip into her ears as would not be too shocking, and was considered a useful minister, at least when he was in his prime. Once he held Victoria's hand, saying he wanted to feel the pulse of England. She thought he had gone too far, especially for a Conservative Liberal.

At that, she liked Lord Melbourne better than Sir Robert Peel, who stirred his tea with his fingers, and Lord Palmerston, who was highhanded. (He had short arms.) But there was no one she could really trust, so she stopped leaning on her Prime Ministers and used a cane.

MARRIAGE TO PRINCE ALBERT

When she was twenty, Victoria felt she should take a husband for the good of her dynasty. She was especially moved by the plight of her cousin, Prince Charles Augustus Albert Emmanuel of Saxe-Coburg-Gotha, who lived in a country too small for his name. Moreover, she liked his looks. He was tall and broad-shouldered, with a Greek nose, blue eyes, delicate mustachios, and fuzzy whiskers that looked as if they wouldn't scratch. Standing stiffly erect in his handsomely braided uniform, he looked like a wooden soldier. Anyway, he looked wooden. To Victoria he seemed a perfect match.

"Prince Charles Augustus Albert Emmanuel of Saxe-Coburg-Gotha," Victoria blurted out. They were seated at opposite ends of a long sofa, and she had to lift her voice to be heard.

"*Ja?*"

"May I call you Prince Albert?"

"*Ja.*"

After such an intimate conversation there was only one honorable thing to do. They trothed.

"May I call you Albert?"

LIFE WITH ALBERT

Albert was a model husband, although his model has long since gone out of fashion. Wherever the royal couple were—at Buckingham Palace, Windsor, or Balmoral—they passed their days in the same happy routine. Twelve hours a day they worked at marble-topped writing tables placed side by side, he drawing plans for the Crystal Palace and she writing pages and pages about "dearest Albert" in her diary. From time to time they stole a glance at each other, and when their eyes met they blushed becomingly.[1] Then they returned to their work, feeling guilty to have taken time from their Sacred Duty to England.

In the evening they would entertain a few Eminent Victorians. First the guests would be allowed one platitude apiece. Then, for a half hour or so, they would look at photograph albums full of pictures of people they didn't know. Precisely at 8:30 everyone would start yawning, the women behind their fans and the men behind their whiskers. On important holidays, like the Fourth of July, Albert might play selections from

[1] At first blush this probably seemed silly, but they got used to it.

Tannhäuser on the organ. Warming up to the occasion, he would pull out all the stops, and consequently had trouble concluding.

Victoria quarreled with Albert only once. This was the famous occasion when he became angry and locked himself in his room. Victoria knocked on the door and asked to come in.

"Who is there?" he asked.

"The Queen of England," she replied.

When he made no move, she knocked harder and furiously demanded entrance.

"Who is there?" again came the question.

Victoria was beginning to catch on. "Your wife, Albert," was her meek reply.

Sentimental biographers such as Lytton Strachey say that, at this point, "the door was immediately opened." However, recent research reveals that a certain Lady Elizabeth Pillowslip, Mistress of the Linen Closet, was coming up the passage just at that moment. She distinctly heard Albert, after a long pause, say firmly and unmistakably, "Skiddoo."[1]

Albert collected art

Albert tried his best to be English, but deep down inside he remained as German as ever. He collected painted porcelain

[1] Defenders of Albert insist that Lady Pillowslip must have been three sheets to the wind.

mustache cups, sat in carved chairs with staghorn legs, sniffed at glass flowers, and kept his *knackwurst* in a Chippendale chest. His room had large-pattern wallpaper, brass fixtures, and heavy draperies. Statuary included a wrought-iron figure representing Enlightenment, which, being completely functional, held aloft a reading lamp. Albert loved art, and it is a pity he had such bad taste.[1]

The only thing about Albert that really distressed Victoria was not his fault. What happened to Lord Chesterfield, to Philip Morris, and to Sir Walter Raleigh happened to Prince Albert. It was a shock to Victoria when she heard that her dear husband was identified with the filthy weed, and that at tobacconists' everywhere men were stepping up to the counter and asking, "Have you Prince Albert in a can?"

WIDOW OF WINDSOR

Albert died at an early age from some mysterious ailment. Some believe he was gradually choked to death by his high collar. After his demise, Victoria shut herself up in Windsor Castle. There had never been a breath of scandal in the place, and now there was hardly a breath of air.[2] It seemed as though she was never coming outdoors again. As the years went by, and England was kept in mourning, the irritation of women began to mount. Many of them began to realize they didn't look their best in black. At last Disraeli got Victoria out by telling her she was needed to help unveil a new statue of Albert.[3]

Disraeli was her favorite Prime Minister during the later years of her reign. She called him Dizzy. It was the only joke Victoria ever made and it convulsed Gladstone, who died. Victoria's attitude toward humor is indicated by her famous utterance: "Under any circumstance, we must have pomp." Sir Edward Elgar set it to music, and Victoria much preferred it to Gilbert and Sullivan.

As the years went by, Victoria began to accumulate all sorts

[1] Victoria never noticed.

[2] The curtains looked drawn, and so did Victoria.

[3] This was the truth. More than five hundred thousand statues of Albert had been unveiled that year, and people had sore arms from pulling ropes.

of precious possessions: chinaware, silver plate, stuffed animals, mugs from her childhood (as well as portraits of her later years), life-sized groups in marble, life-sized marbles in groups, and India. This last was presented to her by Disraeli, along with the title of Empress.[1] He had forgotten to bring a bouquet, and knew she would be expecting *something*.

It has been said of Victoria that she kept "furs, bonnets,

Disraeli's little gift to the Queen—India

muffs, and dresses that she had had for seventy years." It should be added that she not only kept them but wore them. At any rate, she was always neat and clean. There was never a spot on her crinoline or a blot on her escutcheon.

Near the end of her life she had more grandchildren and great-grandchildren than she could crowd into a family portrait. To each grandson who abstained from liquor, tobacco, and loud laughter until he was seventy-five, Victoria promised a throne. By 1890, they were sitting on all the larger thrones of Europe and casting covetous eyes on Monaco and Liechtenstein. It was a Royal Trust; apparently they lacked confidence in anyone who wasn't related.

Queen Victoria's most famous remark occurred when some-

[1] In India, however, she was known as The Brown Man's Burden.

one in court told an indiscreet story while she was holding an audience with Disraeli.

"We are not amused," Victoria said.

It was just like her to include Disraeli. Actually, he thought it was funny as hell.

☞   MORAL: *Drink, smoke, and burn the candle at both ends, because the chances are against your becoming Queen of England anyhow.*

———◆———

CHAPTER XIII

MATA HARI
A SPYING WOMAN

MATA HARI TOLD EVERYONE she was born in India, on the shores of the sacred Ganges, and was an Untouchable. This was an absurd story, but useful on those occasions when she didn't want to be touched. Actually she was born in Holland in 1876, and her name was Margaret Gertrude Zelle.[1] She was always stretching the truth, and eventually got it completely out of shape.

A LITTLE-KNOWN CHILDHOOD INCIDENT

Her mother, Zinfandel Zelle, once said to Mata in a fit of annoyance, "You've made your own bed, now lie in it." Mata

[1] Her father was a plain burgher, without pickles or onions.

126

took this advice to heart and never told the truth after retiring, which perhaps accounts for her extraordinary success as a spy

LIFE IN JAVA

Although Mata Hari was never in India, she learned about the Mysterious East when she married Campbell MacLeod, a captain in the Dutch colonial army, and went with him to Java. There they lived on a coffee plantation, where their incompatibility soon became apparent: she took hers with cream and he took his black! MacLeod, whom she took for a Scot, turned out to be a sot. Drink brought out the worst in him, and she was amazed at how much there was. His only way of sobering up was to beat his wife until he became exhausted, after which he enjoyed a restful sleep. Obviously he was a Scot who deserved to be kilt. She told him he would have to choose between her and drink. His choice was clear, amber-colored, and 90 proof. So she left him and returned to Holland with her two small children, several battered suitcases, and a number of bruises on her trunk.

Her experiences on the plantation in Java turned her against coffee but provided grounds for divorce. As soon as she was free, she headed for the gay life of Paris. After what she had been through, she thought she deserved some fun. She was itching to dance, and those who saw her on the stage thought she must still be itching.

HER CAREER AS A DANCER

Mata Hari soon became the rage of Paris for her exotic dance routine, which, according to her story, she had first performed before the Maharajah of Kanda Swany.[1] Going through her mystic rites in honor of Siva, the sin god, she rolled her large brown eyes, waved her beautiful arms, and passed the hat, simultaneously.

Even more successful than her public performances were her private showings. These were witnessed by learned Orientalists, suave *boulevardiers*, and talent scouts from the Belly

[1] Way down upon the Swany River.

127

Russe. At her special *soirées*, where she did the Dance of the Hundred Veils, she served champagne. Corks were popping and, along about the ninety-ninth veil, so were eyes.

SHE BECOMES A SPY

But all this dancing was only a cover.[1] Mata Hari was in truth a spy for German Intelligence, what there was of it. World War I was on, and the Kaiser was always asking his generals such searching questions as *"Ver haf I mein field glasses putten?"* and *"Bitte schön, vot time it iss?"* (He is said to have turned back the clock, and could never be sure.) Unless they could give him the answers immediately, he would shout *"Dumkopf!"* and strip off two or three rows of iron crosses. They grew desperate. What they needed was someone who could outwit the French and British, especially the French. They had read *Punch* and knew it would be easy enough to outwit the British.

Herr von Jagow, a high-placed government official (he lived on the sixth floor of the Hotel Adlon), thought of just the per-

[1] Many times it was all she had.

son. He had been sharing the favors of Mata Hari, then visiting in Berlin, with the Prussian Crown Prince, three barons, and a field marshal,[1] and thought she would make a perfect spy. She had long ears for eavesdropping, long fingers for pickpocketing, and high cheekbones for good measure. Moreover, she seemed to know every Tom, Dick, and Hari. Her dancing had given her a catlike tread, indispensable to secret agents, *saboteurs,* and cats. When von Jagow asked her whether she had the necessary courage to become a spy, she ground out a cigarette in the palm of his hand to show her contempt for pain.

What motivated Mata Hari to take up a career in which there was nothing but excitement, easy money, and, if she should be caught, everlasting fame? Who knows? But it is not for us to tarry long over the Enigmas of History. Suffice it to

The generals were favorably impressed

say that the German High Command, a group of six-footers, inspected Mata Hari one at a time (they had only a single monocle among them), and were favorably impressed. They promised her a house, so she threw in her lot.

[1] Mata Hari was always doing people favors.

After an intensive course at the Imperial School for Spies, where she majored in Sinister Activities, wrote a brilliant thesis in a code which none of her instructors could crack, and gave the valedictory address on "Counter Spying at Cafeterias," she took her B.S. (Bachelor of Spying) and returned to Paris. She carried with her the tools of the trade: kid gloves for hiding fingerprints and handling suspicious police, a six-inch cigarette holder,[1] a flask of strong perfume for throwing people off the scent, a book of judo instructions for throwing people off the cliff, binoculars (i.e., spy glasses), a large empty bottle full of invisible ink, and a wardrobe of black silk dresses three sizes too small.

ESPIONAGE AND INTRIGUE

Back in Paris, Mata Hari set up shop in an expensive villa, and prepared to become a villaness. Her place of business was completely equipped. There were panels that slid back at the drop of a hat (as soon as the hatrack got too crowded), mirrors that were really windows and windows that were really mirrors, pipelines from the French Cabinet (usually full of brandy), and a small printing press in the basement for turning out counterfeit money, forged passports, and timetables of the Allied advance.[2]

Mata Hari's technique was to go to a fashionable café and sit at a table alone, sipping wine, puffing a cigarette held in her long holder, and transmitting the menu over the short-wave radio concealed in her handbag. (The Kaiser loved French food.) When she got the eye of a government official or an Army officer, she would give him a sidelong glance [3] and drop her napkin. The gentleman would usually pick up her napkin and find her check folded inside. On one occasion the gentleman turned out to be a spy from Holland, so they decided to go Dutch.

That evening her new acquaintance would be an audience of one in Mata Hari's drawing room, watching a dance from the

[1] With a built-in ash tray and warning whistle.
[2] Complete with asterisks and small type for Sundays and holidays.
[3] To either side, and as long as necessary.

Far East (but sitting up close) and feeling like a Maharajah. After the performance, Mata would usually open a conversation with such a gambit as "What's new?" or "What do you know?" She was an excellent listener. Moreover her photographic mind had no need for flash bulbs when working in the dark.

Mata Hari had an uncanny sense for selecting her victims, being able to tell a general, even in civilian clothes, by the way he ordered his food, and a diplomat by the laundry marks on his spats. The only time she was misled was when she enticed an epauleted gentleman to her drawing room, thinking him a British Admiral. He turned out to be the hotel doorman, and the best she could get for her evening's work was the secret plans to the mop closet.

Mata's mistake

Mata Hari had a weakness for young Army officers. By the end of her first year in business she had a collection of trench coats second only to the French Quartermaster's. Even the Chief of the French Ministry of Foreign Affairs was snagged in her net. He generously let her send messages out of the country in diplomatic pouches, right under the eyes of dissipated ambassadors. Not that they didn't suspect her. Sometimes in her audiences as she danced were French secret agents, watching her every move. But they had to admit that nothing could be pinned on her.

Soon the Germans had her prying into such military secrets as the disposition of the French troops. (She reported that they could be mighty grumpy and unpleasant.) One of her missions was to discover the reason for their nonchalance in the face of danger. When they saw the Germans approaching with drawn bayonets, they would say "Bosh."

Mata Hari loved her work, and would spend her days off memorizing unnecessary telephone numbers and learning to speak distinctly with a map of the Paris metro pasted to the roof of her mouth. If she ever went to the beach, it was only to see whether the coast was clear.

The only thing that worried Mata was that the war might end and there would be a slump in the espionage business. To guard against such an eventuality, she took a correspondence course in more dependable civilian pursuits, such as shop lifting [1] and safe cracking.

SPYING FOR THE GERMANS AND/OR FRENCH

At length the French grew suspicious. Their army was reduced to impotence, the brains of the General Staff having been left at Mata Hari's villa, along with gloves, capes, swagger sticks, and *képis*. A group of French officers, annoyed because they had never been invited, made a raid while she was in the midst of a dance. Immediately they were satisfied on one count: she was carrying no concealed weapons. The raiding party ran their fingers over the walls, trying to find secret panels, but picked up nothing but splinters. It being an old wooden house, their search failed to turn up any concrete evidence.

Realizing that her bread could be buttered on both sides, Mata Hari enlisted as a spy for the French. Henceforth she

[1] At first she could lift only a small shop, but got so she could hoist the corner of the Galeries Lafayette.

spied for the Germans on Monday, Wednesday, and Friday and for the French on Tuesday, Thursday, and Saturday. Sunday was set aside for keeping two sets of books.

She kept two sets of books

Some biographers aver that Mata Hari was a woman without moral scruples or conscience. They overlook the meticulous way in which she gave exactly fifty per cent of her time to each side. When her books failed to balance at the end of the month, she would go out in any weather or at any hour of the night to do a little extra spying for the French or the Germans, as might be required.

CAUGHT AT LAST

One day, however, the French intercepted an innocent-looking letter to the German General Staff. On the surface it was merely pleasantries about French artillery positions and the plans for a new British tank. But when the French cryptographers held the letter up to the light, they could see through it all. She was transmitting to the Germans a centuries-old recipe for onion soup. She had gone too far. . . .

Mata Hari was given a summery court martial (it was late June), condemned to death by a firing squad, and thrown into prison to await the fatal hour.

In her prison cell she demanded the luxuries to which she was accustomed: soft cushions, soft music, soft lights, soft soap. One of her requirements was a daily bath in milk, and she sat impatiently in the tub each morning waiting for the milkman. The day before her execution she was permitted the luxury of cream. To the last, she was unperturbed, feeling confident that the members of the firing squad would be unable to hold their rifles steady when they sighted their target.

On the day of her execution she was awakened early and given a *filet mignon* breakfast while her guards, who were used to *croissants* and coffee, looked on hungrily. Granted permission to do one last dance, to get the kinks out after long confinement, she writhed sinuously until told the jig was up.

As for the execution, it went off without incident. At one point, it is true, thirty rifles cracked. They were old equipment, left over from the Franco-Prussian War, and were speedily replaced.

Mata Hari's plans to distract her executioners went awry. The French officers knew their men. They blindfolded not Mata Hari but the firing squad.

☞   Moral: *What idiot said Heaven help the working girl?*

134

EPILOGUE

LOOKING BACK over, under, and between the great women of the past, one notices some interesting similarities. Consider, for example, Delilah and Mata Hari, both of whom wormed secrets out of men; Eve, before the Fall, and Lady Godiva, before the cold weather; Madame de Pompadour and Delilah, both of them preoccupied with hair; Elizabeth and Victoria, both of them English; and Helen of Troy and Catherine the Great, both of them women.

Looking at the outstanding women of our own day, one wonders whether they are the equal of the great women so faithfully described in these pages, and whether future historians will similarly do them justice. Admittedly, the chopping block of the Tudors and the poisons of the Borgias are now rarely used, but have not subtler methods of torture been developed? Fewer women are on thrones, but is this not because there are fewer thrones? And are there not new points of vantage from which to harass men?

This raises interesting questions about the whole concept of the *femme fatale*. Is she a woman who shakes empires, or just men? Does she become *fatale* only after death? Does she require generations of imaginative historians to magnify her proportions and multiply her accomplishments? Perhaps if the important women of today are not recognized as *femmes fatales*, it is because a little perspective is needed. Looking at a woman of our own time is like looking at an oil painting up too close; seen from a distance, the true meaning dawns on us. In a few hundred years, the great women of the twentieth century will be known for what they are, but it will be too late to do anything about it.

This is not the last word, or even the next-to-last word, on the subject. The author admits that his history of women is not so much definitive as it is suggestive. But if he has not given the full sweep of history, he has at least given the sweepings.

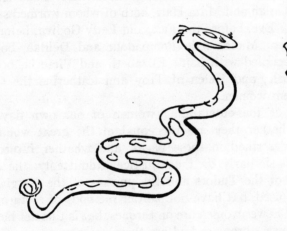

ABOUT THE AUTHOR

Richard Armour draws upon unusual resources in writing about women: his mother is a woman, his wife is a woman, his daughter will soon be a woman, and he teaches at a college for women. As befits a man who has done extensive research for the present volume, he leads a double life. In fact he leads a double life several times over: as a college professor and a writer, as a writer of serious works and humor, and as a writer of light verse and even lighter prose. He was born in San Pedro, California, in 1906. After taking his Ph.D. at Harvard, teaching at such institutions as the University of Texas, Northwestern University, Wells College, and the University of Freiburg, and serving for four years in the Army, he returned to his native state, where he is now Professor of English at Scripps College and the Claremont Graduate School.

As a scholar, he has written books of biography and literary criticism and taught or held research fellowships in England, France, and Germany. He is a book reviewer for newspapers and a member of the editorial staff of several magazines. A prolific light-verse writer, he has contributed several thousand verses to magazines in the United States and England. Many of these have been collected in such volumes as *Light Armour*. More recently he has gained a wide readership for his best-selling spoofs of history, *It All Started with Columbus* and *It All Started with Europa*, in which learning and laughter mingle. Scholar-humorist Armour lives with his wife and two children in Claremont, California.